HOUSING HIGHER CONSCIOUSNESS

VIBRATE TO 360 SENSES

This book is produced
In the United States of America
For the Higher Vibrations of the World,
Mother Earth, and all her inhabitants.

This is a work of nonfiction.
All rights reserved.

Published by: Vibrate Higher Productions
vibratehigher.eth | vibratehigher.nft
reinanatasha.com
©Vibrate Higher Productions

Cover Design: R.N.K.
Inside Art: R.N.K.
Layout Artist: R.N.K.
Editor: Donna Erriah / R.N.K.
Printed by: Vibrate Higher Productions
Title: Reza Zulmi Serif
Handwriting: Distant Stroke
Node Headings: 16 pt Palatino
Node Name Headings: Distant Stroke
Text set: 10 pt Palatino

Names: R.N.K., Reina Natasha, Reena Natasha Khilawan
Title: Housing Higher Consciousness - Vibrate to 360 Senses
R.N.K. / Reina Natasha / Reena Natasha Khilawan;
copy editor: Donna Danamah Erriah
Description: First Edition | California
ISBN 978-0-578-29114-7
Vibrate Higher Productions, 2022
Subjects: Spirituality | Mysticism | Vibrations | Universe

Immense Gratitude

Divine Mother Earth

Tipsy Kay

Donna Danamah Erriah

Dorian Johnson

Dedication

For *Mother Gaia, Prakriti, Mother Nature,*
I am grateful and honored for breathing in your guidance and exhaling your truth. I live in surrender. I bow down in gratitude.

For my soul-guide and eternal furry friend, *Tipsy Kay,*
Your unconditional Love lives in my heart.

For my Aunty, my luminescence editor, and first reader, *Donna Danamah Erriah,*
Your sublime intelligence and unconditioned Love are unmatched. Immense gratitude lives in my heart for your patience in hours, days, weeks, and months of edits with me. YOU have given ME the gift of your TIME, timeless. You have artistically and vibrationally enhanced my craft that propels these words into the Universe. This is OUR imprint.

For my musical soulmate and fellow light-worker, *Dorian Johnson,*
Thank you for seeing my light, and believing in the sounds that transcend through me.

For my *Mother,*
Your luminosity radiates the awakening of my soul code. Through your sacred womb, I have learned "*OHM*", the Primordial Sound.

For my *Father,*
Forever am I grateful that you have shown me the practice of discipline and focus.

For my Sister *Diana Monique,*
Thank you for your lifelong encouragement, and for the growth that we have experienced on this life journey.

For my Nephew *Ayden Jay*

For my Brother *John Darwin*

For my *Elders and Ancestors*

For all of my *Family*

For the *Matriarchy Rising*

For all the *Warriors* that have Arrived, and honor their quest as light-workers.

For all of the *Mothers and Fathers,*
Raising the **next gen** *Queens and Kings.*

For all Souls that seek liberation

Note to Reader

The information and thought processes shared in this book are for information purposes only. The information shared is not to be used for the indoctrination of humanity. Enlightenment is harnessed by the intelligence for conscious living and awareness in the body, mind, and soul vibration. Although the experiences of others in their quest for *Housing Higher Consciousness* may aid in your own path of exploration, your own experiences are always unique. The perceptions and experiences regarding psychedelics and plant medicine are shared for perspective only, and do not serve as advice for experimental usage or seeking liberation. You are the master of your mind and body programming for awakening the soul code. Please consult and believe in yourself before taking advice from others. May these words guide YOU to higher vibrational frequencies for *Housing Higher Consciousness* that *Vibrate to 360 Senses*.

Vibrate Higher,
R.N.K.

Nodes

Node 1

Intro [applied]

Dear Light-workers of the Universe,

You are seeking and I welcome you with open arms, an open heart, and endless Love. Our souls have roamed dimensions, a long journey through countless realms. Remember, you are one with Mother Earth. Gaia is Higher Consciousness. Through *Housing Higher Consciousness*, humanity remembers their magic. Your soul is calling to return to the realm of infinite possibilities. Meditation, plant intelligence, conscious vibrations, art forms, and the creation of new patterns for an empathetic world are breathing through you. Your soul yearns to reconnect consciously to the primordial spirals.

Through interconnected guidance, I have compiled my messages and vibrations into words to help guide, honor belief in the self, and remember the patterns of the Earth. Gaia is my employer. I surround myself with the sounds of her wind, the waves of her oceans, and the magic of her mountains. The Nodes in this nanoscopic compilation of *Housing Higher Consciousness* reveal messages gifted to me by the Earth and her sacred geometry. The title of each Node corresponds to a specific song from my musical album, *Like Psychedelics*. The lyrics of each song culminate with its corresponding Node.

Endless contributions from Mother Nature have gifted me spiritual guidance. I have been blessed with spiritual teachers in my life. One of my spiritual teachers was Tipsy Kay, my dog, and Guru. Tipsy manifested unconditional Love in my life, and countless adventures that led to my awakening.

Love, empathy, the awakening of humanity and free-spirit, married with the dance of growth and freedom, **power my art**. The microcosm and celestial bodies create the endless movement of spirals and possibilities. Even as microcosmic and celestial particles, conscious phenomena are our dance with the Universe. The missions I take on, and everything forthcoming, is a guide. **May you look beyond this civilization's presentations.** Gratitude and self-expression are the results

Intro (applied)

of my growth. Through soul activation, I have discovered my honor to the Universe. My soul code has guided me to honor the sacred work of Gaia. In this same breath, the soul code facilitates the unlearning of old patterns and habits that control the Avatar. My persistent elevation and constant practice of *Vibrating to 360 Senses* have transcended the wording of *Housing Higher Consciousness.*

May these words help you on your journey through the creative realms, hearts, and inner wiring, which are our connectors to Mother Earth. May you steer free from ego-based consciousness and greed-induced experiences. May you sow your seeds and reap soul activation as a light-worker on planet Earth.

May you find wisdom through believing in YOU and freeing yourself from improvidence, and negation of the microcosm. May these words guide you to be the ruler of a genuine and empathetic world by honoring the Divine, the inventor, the creator, and the Higher Being that YOU are. **You have missions; may they be unleashed!**

R.N.K.

Intro (applied)

Intro (applied)

I don't want to be
Programmed (beyond code)
Is it helping me?

Finally, I'm here
Warrior Arrived
Next gen Queens and Kings

World of Pulsation
Enter vibration
Self-domination

I am here
For the **Matriarchy Rising**
Through self-elevation

Yes,
Trusting in me
Binary Humans
Can't take over me
The soul **Inner Compass**
Is life of the tree
And the tree of our life
That will give energy
And the energy tracing
The things that I need

Vibrating Higher
Through deep frequencies
Practicing Dharma *and also to leave*
The bad energy that is given to me

I can only do the things I Love
I can't waste my breath
I call **Euphoria**
Awakening *my light*
Awakening my soul
Dharma *cross-***Applied** *this light*
Solitude *needs more*
Releasing *every moment*
Where the pain had hit me low
Right below the belt
But now my Goddess calls it **Growth**
And she gave me **Freedom**
And she gave me light
Soul Sex *reaching states*
Every single night

(practice)
(applied)

Node 2

Like Psychedelics

~Mayavi Davayi~

R.N.K.

Travel with me for a brief moment to the time when I discovered **plant intelligence**. If it is your first time hearing this term, it is just what the words say. It is the intelligence of plants. In 2011, someone, from a random encounter, explained their experience with N,N-Dimethyltryptamine (DMT) to me. Entheogens contain DMT, which is also a natural endogenous compound found in plants, animals, and humans. Strangely, this is deemed an illegal substance by human regulations. Due to the altering of states and unpredictable, profound experiences, this compound is illegal in most places. During elevation, DMT releases through a natural onset activation of the pineal gland. This gland is located 1.5 inches inward from the middle of the forehead. This gland is the producer of DMT within our bodies. However, the DMT extracts from nature or DMT synthesis are deemed illegal. DMT (also referred to as the "God molecule") is the intelligence and Higher Consciousness of humans, plants, and animals. It is a neurotransmitter that connects all species in Nature. Learning this general information ignited my curiosity. My research of scriptures, books, journals, and documentaries enlightened my knowledge. However, my divine entrance into Higher Consciousness happened with my profound but ancient understanding of plant intelligence, Nature's law, cosmic vibrations, cosmic law, and cosmic scolding. I became aware that my divine entrance was not absolute. The Divine cannot be understood through the perspective of others. Instead, the answers would come through the unfolding of divine timing and alignment. Walking my spiritual path would impart divine timing.

In 2013, one of my divine awakenings manifested. It felt otherworldly. The moment happened in Palos Verdes, California. I have lived around bountiful nature since my move to the United States. Most days in Southern California are breathtaking and this particular day was nothing short of this. It was a gorgeous day with clear blue skies and the piercing visuals of Mother Nature. I had just gone through the tremendous loss of two of my grandparents. We find ourselves going through new layers of grief when we are living away from our loved ones. The experience of loss is always a tough pill to swallow. The mind finds new ways of coping when going through mourning and grief. Nature does its wonders in those moments when the body takes on a shock. Tail wagging Tipsy and I decided to take a drive down to the ocean side. We went down some steps that led to the ocean and stood by the ridge. Peeking over the cliff, I observed leaves from trees and sea moss swaying back and forth, and waves crashing against the rocks. An epiphany suddenly took place. Pure bliss overcame me as I listened to my heart beating calmly. Suddenly, what seemed like a wave of diamond dust fell from the sky. It covered Tipsy, my skin, and all of my surroundings. Diamond dust! Perhaps there was some disbelief taking place in my brain. Is this really happening? Is this a trip? There was no explanation.

The next day, I revisited this breathtaking place and went down those steps to the ridge again. Tipsy was on a leash and made his way towards a tree. I had to redirect him as I stood there and gazed at a Buddhist Monk sitting under a tree. He faced the ocean and used this view as his prayer point. I could not decipher the messages from what I had witnessed on both days. What occurred was something of a higher awakening and a call to divine alignment. This day manifested the conception of my musical album, *Like Psychedelics*. A song, composed on that day, sat in my creation vault for five years, before it shifted me to create a musical body in the form of an album.

Five years thenceforth, I was blessed with the introduction to "Mayavi Davayi," the elusive reset of Gaia. Mayavi Davayi is Hindi for "Elusive Medicine". This would be my first experience with psychedelics, and a glance into the fungi networks. It would help me understand access and activation to my inner world, healing, and the profound path to my missions on Earth. The magic mushroom called me and appeared through divine timing and alignment. It felt perfect and surreal simultaneously. I recall the sound of the herb grinder crushing the "Golden Teacher" mushrooms which were steeped into a tea, and poured in a wooden cup. Surrendered to my non-programmed state and with zero expectations, I drank my entheogenic magic mushroom tea.

It is important to mention that one cannot predict what transpires when psychedelics activate the Third Eye. Discovery and understanding occurs after and perhaps lingers for as long as we live. We learn through these gateways, but how we learn and what we "see" is personal to our journey. It may help to sit in silence through meditation and seek the focus of "Mantras", positive recited words. Drinking this entheogenic tea already indicated this would be transformational to my life. It took a moment for the mushrooms to sync with my soul code. A fellow psychonaut, my beloved furry friend, Tipsy and I took a brief nature walk along a canyon. I felt nature "come to life" on that particular walk. In one moment it felt as if the branches and bushes parted and when this happened I stood locked in deep eye contact with a Deer! It was magical! Nature danced and revealed its endless layers. I felt my body getting heavier and knew I had to get back to my home "setting" to lay down. At this point, the inner journey started through dimensions and realm travels. My first recollection is the sacredness of tapping into the cosmic vibrations, "Nature's network". The sacred self-similarity network activates the Third Eye—a fall into the Universe's intense and deep layer stack. The activation dilates the pupils and brings the mind to stillness. The activation also has a focus on moving energies which would teach me to surrender. Surrender is unlearning every philosophy and complexity of life, with intentions of learning anew. With a receptive and warming heart, I yielded to the internal vibration. In return, the Universe stripped my fears.

Sensory modalities perceived music as dancing vibrational colors. The realms calculated sacred geometry, while I watched these calculations in real-time, and unfolded the magic of the Universe. I visually conceived the different levels of Euphoria. Patterns communicated distant strangers, spiritual teachers, and their memories of astral travel in prayer and meditation. Pastel clouds presented the gateway of heaven. My heart experienced the glows of vivid purple colors through my frontal cortex, which connected me to everything. Nature calmly breathed in and out auras. The mushrooms that seemed to dance around in the realms communicated without language, but I understood. The mushrooms welcomed me and vibrationally communicated to each other, "She's here!, She's here!". This unequivocally made me smile. Everything in Nature spoke and I understood that Mother Nature gifted downloads and uploads through the microcosm. Neurons fired and wired through geometric, sophisticated, magnificent, and empathetic patterns. I knew I had returned to this magical place countless times before. Suddenly, I cried profound tears that communicated ancestral life paths with intervals of highs and lows, and the healing of ancestral trauma. Tears flowed from my face for my loved ones, which was a complete and complex release, and therapy of a lifetime. As sunset approached on that awe-inspiring day, I exited the dimensions with a lifetime of terabytes in uploads and downloads. My soul-print was activated and ready to further unfold Higher Consciousness. There are no realm manuals, but I learned that energy decodes through self-trust and self-similarity network patterns.

Synesthesia amplifies the auditory and visual range of frequency on the sacred geometry field. The vibration is ego-less; the opposite is the greed that prevails here on Earth today. The pulse of Nature serves the collective and worldly vibration, starting with the self. Our human civilization will seem insane through cosmic law. We will never know what is possible unless we go beyond our preconditions. Psychedelics, in their entirety, are ineffable as hinted in this passage. Although my experimenting has extended to many more experiences, this first journey was indubitably an entrance to understanding a fraction of the microcosmic gateways.

A few days after my entheogenic journey, I met with my longtime friend and musical soulmate, Dorian Johnson. We had lost touch for a few years. Creativity had hit a back-burner as I navigated my divine alignment. However, meeting Dorian again after all this time, sparked a flame of inventive artistry. During our meal, we exchanged stories and vibrations, including my psychedelic experience. I abruptly announced that I would be deploying a musical album. This body of work would have the name, *Like Psychedelics*, and it would have eighteen songs (eventually becoming twenty). Dorian looked at me and listened. Reaching a pause during my impromptu rant, I asked him, "Will you exec produce it?" And he exclaimed, "Let's do it! I'm ready!". I felt alive and courageous. I was manifesting bigger and bolder than anything that could have formed through explicitly laying out a plan. Dorian was not just a person in my life. He was a manifested light-worker, who emitted light, and found my ray of light in the dark. My journey paved a new trajectory. This would become the path to *Housing* my *Higher Consciousness*.

Like Psychedelics

I'm such a tease
You're such a flirt

Streaming through my head
Like the other night
Second chance
Might knock reality
Out of sight
Cosmo spinning
Lighting dancing
Right in front of me
This can't be anything
The bare eyes can see
Euphoric levels running right
Through my veins
And human nature
Does seem a bit insane
And DMT just floated
In and out of my brain
I can't catch anything
That you wanted to say

Guide me through the realm
Pattern overflow
Glowing in existence
Show me what I need to know

I'm such a tease
You're such a flirt

Mayavi Davayi

Touch me while I'm dancing
Touch me while I'm singing
Shine while I'm undressing
And you're always winning
Yeah, you do it to the lovers in the world
But I'm alone with you
And my head is slowly spinning
As you keep my secrets
You know how to get me naked
Strip me down
Until I'm warmly faded
Naked as I lay there faded
Naked as I lay there faded

Streaming through my head
Like the other night
Second chance might knock reality
Out of sight
Cosmo spinning
Lighting dancing
Right in front of me
This can't be anything
The bare eyes can see
Euphoric levels running right

Like Psychedelics

Through my veins
And human nature
Does seem a bit insane
And DMT just floated
In and out of my brain
I can't catch anything
That you wanted to say

I'm right here
Where the Goddess
Gave my pain away
To souls who
Choose to live that way
And I will not
Look back that way
I give up on
The things you say
And everything
Makes more sense that way
And the only thing
That can change this play
Is when the truth is set
And bound to stay

I'm such a tease
You're such a flirt

Mayavi Davayi

Node 3

Programmed

[beyond code]

~Fear is not real~

The soul-print maps the original cosmic state before societal programming. Once the microcosm state is unlocked, there is no return to unlearning this state. Humans rely on the education of their civilization to advance to a better world. However, education is also the societal programming that leads the world to chase finances and succeed, within the structure. Imagine if the entire human race believed in themselves, and strived to help each other from mere wisdom. On a smaller scale, this wisdom would benefit the direct environment of individuals, and their connections to each other and the Earth. On a larger scale, it would alter the competitive behaviors that can lead to countless threats of dogmatic wars and weapons of mass destruction. Raising the human vibration is not the accumulation of things and working for the external entity. The vibration is raised through the accumulation of consciousness and working for the collective. Humanity fights over resources and land, yet both exist with or without them. External entities claim but cannot "own" land, for the land belongs to the Earth. If it is truly believed and accepted that land belongs to this planet, nature raises in vibration. When the vibration is raised the Earth gives back abundance to its inhabitants. A decentralized and collective effort from Nature provides necessities for humans, despite their circumstances and Earth's empathetic exertion. The growth of food is not attached to the classification of rich or poor, as it relates to humans. The human race is capable of inventing for a higher civilization, loving Mother Nature, and caring for all of her inhabitants, empathetically. Respecting Earth activates consciousness that is awakened at birth.

Imagine that you are a plant residing in the forest where your ecosystem has four seasons, and where all growing conditions are met. Mother Nature provides water and sunlight at intervals. You are an intelligent plant that is growing in all your complexity and are using the wisdom of the companion plants that are growing around you. You are growing in your original state. You are encoding your needs for survival from your surrounding Eco. Now, imagine that you are a resourceful plant to the economy of the human-made world. You are pushed out of nature's

network and placed in regulated air and grounds. The complexity of your growth stagnates compared to the wisdom in the growth of a forest plant. Due to demand for your kind, the network needs to adjust to predictable conditions. These modifications encapsulate the network. You are no longer the original plant from the forest. Relearning to root into Gaia would take time. It will need to replenish, drain, change seasons, and reinforce native growth conditions. This plant example demonstrates that the world can either be your forest or your Genetically Modified Organism (GMO) garden.

Consciousness requires practice and discipline. Feeding the mind-body system requires eliminating toxins, and piecing together a new mind-body program. This new program may sound laborious in this world where big Pharma, processed foods, and mental programming rule human's mystical bodies. The old body program feeds the economy by modifying the mind-body system. The modifications just patch medicine dependent bodies and prolong chronic illnesses. When medicines that are deemed safe are used, side effects can resurface and cause new ailments over time. Imagine the unseen harm on the human body when it is GMO'd. Mother Nature and her growing network power human consciousness. The new body program relies on her network to breathe, think, eat, work, and operate without human interference. Before taking care of anyone, the mind needs to be nurtured in order to gain universal receptors to think beyond the self, family, friends, social norms, governed minds, lands, and countries. **Serving the Universe as a planet, endlessly and timelessly, plugs into your unified receptors.** The trapped mind lives in a centralized system. Small groups of humans create authority to impose decisions in the lives of others. Everything requires money in this centralized system— including all religious systems. Believing in an organized entity that is structured by humans, requires followers to live, reach, and succeed in a box. Higher Consciousness is all religions linked by chain-connecting events. Fighting over this is superfluous. Ancient scriptures relate stories of a particular time. There is no human to confirm or claim absolute truth to what nature, religion or the realms impart. All scriptures should guide and point humans to live in harmony, tranquility, and in tune with Mother Earth. In return, Gaia is considerate to humans. Interpretations of ancient scriptures are words brilliantly used by those that see an opportunity for greed and deception. There is no one way to live; there are endless ways to live. Those who strive to manipulate mind-control inflict fear on the one-way-of-living notion to keep followers controlled by the chase of money, status, and power. Conditioned lands and ownerships develop a mental slave race, and is the host of mind-control. Division is the source of the mental slave race in game-like governed lands. The worship of money, beliefs, power, policy, self-interpreted religion, and competition turns a blind eye to Nature. This is when humans joined the slave race. There are no straight forward answers on this pathway. However, new nodes are created by nurturing High Vibrations and self-awareness. Changing the world demands a change of energy. Self-transformation charges energy. **With this mindset, a new pulse takes place; one where YOU are guiding—a pulse where you understand your power, path, and missions.**

It starts with our temple and what we consume, for our mindset will struggle when governed and ruled.

Programmed (beyond code)

I picture the world as small
As it sits in the Universe
My movement
My Impact
Greed and Ego
People and Potential
Fear is not real
Who is this Goddess of my mind?
Can she always come to my rescue?
Can I keep her
And create Freedom
And spread light with her?
She heals
We are one
We are Warriors

They programmed the world
To think peace is not real
And the message is simple
You're numbers to change
And I can't stress enough
We're zero's and one's
And the clear fives and sevens
Will hit us like blunts
Starts with our temple
And what we consume

For our mindset will struggle
When governed and ruled
Stay on your toes
They prescribe you the dose
What is made by white coats
Blue collars will boast
And religion is beauty
It's people for evil
Words are interpreted
Guess and primeval
If only we knew
Bout' the things we could do
We would join our forces
And power this through
But the world is not ready
So we start our missions
And I quit my job to
Smart Contract missions
You should be out there
Fulfilling your mission
Guidance of Love
Won't face competition.

I will not give my soul to you.
I will be free from what you do.
Guiding everyone in rows
And I know
If I let go
I'll end up back in the row
So...

Programmed [beyond code]

I'll practice to let go
Let go of ego
So I have clear visions
Rock those vibrations
No invitation
Done with the reference
Financial Obsession
With assets and liquids
The source of depression
All of this stress
Is the source of depression
Exchange tool is worshiped
Where is the lesson?

We're gonna need some answers...

I think it's fundamental
For you to know that
You can reprogram yourself
Because right now
We're basically

Programmed (beyond code)

Node 4

Warriors Arrived

[let them know we have arrived]

~Warrior, listen~

There is a message that repeats in life when light-workers are not journeying through their higher self. It is the calling to honor their highest missions while in their Earth suit. It does not matter how many times someone lets go of their missions in their lifetime. The missions inevitably nestle back into existence. It is the main component of constant energy flow followed by the nurtured concept of light exchange. The nature of soul-work invariably follows the soul to the exit of the Earth suit. Persistent with tasks, the missions reserve light circulating back into the body, reminding the soul of its calling. This understanding helps the stagnation of energy circulation. Luminosity lives within the microcosm, traveling within the mental and physical perpetual states of transformation.

The inner warrior and the higher self are synonymous. The inner warrior operates at a dull baseline when it functions in a role other than the higher self. In this drab role, the warrior is kaleidoscopic, disguised, desolate, dehydrated, unhappy, self-inflicted, and conditioned by its surroundings. The warrior, at the dull baseline, needs a peaceful environment to awaken to their higher self. The warrior takes on roles as Mother, Father, wife, husband, sibling, relative, partner, and friend in this dimensional capacity. The warrior knows that all the assumed roles are guides that lead from within. The warrior absorbs and manifests that the inner Goddess/God is living in a well-housed system that flows with Nature's vibration. The inner Divine is one with the higher self. It unleashes the inner warrior to go beyond their programming, titles, and societal algorithms. Therefore, when getting ready to House Higher Consciousness, the rules, regulations, and claimed ownership of humans disappear in proximity with the inner Divine. The mind-body program is understood by governing entities that seek to control minds. Once we realize that we can reprogram our brain and ways of thinking, a new and healthy perspective is adopted.

Mother Nature, for example, has inhabitants that govern her resources. She has endured cycles of time, spanning billions of years. Humans conquer and claim the Earth. They build, claim ownership and fight on her land. They mass destroy, abuse her inhabitants, and greed her resources. Colorful flags and logos are used to claim ownership of lands. Mother Nature is, however, the ruler of all. She comes in indestructible forms and power, which no army, human-made law, or religion can overthrow. Every nanosecond, we depend on her and her resources to keep us alive. Gaia, however, cannot counter human laws with cases and lawsuits. She strikes back in other ways to claim her land and her Earth. In the same way, the warriors need to fight to claim their minds and bodies that are governed by human laws.

In life, there is no easy road. However, equipped with the unlocked microcosm and profound knowledge, life becomes purposeful. Fortunately, this intermingles with ease. Legendary warriors were wired with resilience to navigate mental processes and battle programmed thoughts. They advocated freedom and adamantly held their ground after receiving "no" for an answer. They were unstoppable and fervent in their quest for liberation. Warriors paved this path thousands of years ago. Imprints of messages continue to awaken inner warriors in the direction of peace and liberty. **Wherever you are in the network of warriors, you are needed to actively participate in the most critical mission in your lifetime. Warriors Arrived, serving Gaia.** Those that try to destroy her

Earth pay their price. Gaia is empathetic when her inhabitants take care of her resources. Humans are the inhabitants of her magnificent and magical Nature that take care of her soul.

One must impart their higher vibrational knowledge to those that are receptive. Higher vibrational knowledge connects to the soul code of the body. The programmable world corrupts this soul code. Therefore, it is important to defy this culprit. The unmodified soul code is active in children, since their gateways to the microcosm have only recently entered the programmable world. The lingering energy and vibrations of the warriors, who arrived thousands of years ago, surround and give reminiscence to the capability of human nature. A switch in the human system activates this energy field. Humans naturally know about this energy field which attracts those on the collective missions and, in turn, wakes up the mind, body, and soul. The mind-body-soul code moves according to the collective missions. Energy flows to parts of the brain, activating missions for the visitation to planet Earth. The inner warrior is a leader and a servant, which places it in a unique decentralized position within the network. Humans are all equally responsible for the light that beams throughout the network. The mission is to help warriors tap into their inner light and collectively perform their sacred tasks. These tasks are neglected in many human traits, which turned empathy for each other into impatience, envy, and anger. No warrior is alike. Avatars, missions, and the gateways of unlocked neurons differentiate. The differences create a perfect puzzle in the corresponding energy field where all earthlings breathe, live, and connect.

What a crazy thought to be fighting for your rights. The fight to control your body, gender, skin color, race, peace, education, food, life, and Love created a marching society. The fight to control free and non-negotiable things is continuous. Humans have taken control of your journey on Earth. You have the power to unite and create an empathetic world with your warrior capabilities. In doing so, you are saving the human race and receiving guidance from Mother Earth. Help each other invent and develop outside of the regulated and centralized resources. Innovations that respect Nature enhance human life. Your brain should not be exhausted from fighting the centralized network. Wake up with ease to your life's missions which power your network with energy. This energy flow will propel you to create. Creativity does not flow with stress, anxiety or a heavy heart; it flows with Nature's vibration. The vibration of Nature is grand and you are this calling. You are the Warrior that has Arrived!

Warriors Arrived (let dem know we have arrived)

Warriors Arrived
Warriors, Vibrate Higher

Open up my heart
Shine my light
I'll walk with you brave
Baby, shine real bright
What you, what I, need to hear
And all of the world
I will show you warriors
Grown from Baby Girls

They raised the Prince, the King, the Pharaoh
No need to bow for a man
Don't make anyone think you owe
Grow
Constantly grow your inner light
Don't make anyone take that from you
Grow your inner light

Warrior,
You're my warrior

Warrior, Listen
Understand your gift in repetition
Know that there's more to your ambition
There will storms but you can make that glisten

You're on a mission
Keep vision
Empower those that listen
Don't form the constant friction
Your body, your decision
Don't make them tell you any different
They're gonna tell you 'You are trippin''
When you form the coalition
And you guide the mass to listen
They wanna format your partition
Don't let them touch your vision
And I tell you this right now
You're in control
Your inner light
You shine so bright
You're gonna fight
You have the right
You will unite
Warrior

Warrior
You're my warrior

Warriors Arrived
Thousands of years ago
We are what this world needs
Bring change to every rule and platform
Let them know we have Arrived!

Open up my heart
To shine my light
I'll walk with you brave
Baby, shine real bright
What you, what I, need to hear
And all of the world
I will show you warriors
Grown from Baby Girls

Warrior this I know
You're the ruler of your world
There's no one
That will get your shine
Walk away
When the Love turns blind
Don't let them pay you any less
Don't let them pay you with their stress
Just to fight for equal pay
Take your brain and walk away
And look inside to what is needed from you now
When your inner Goddess speaks
She will tell you this somehow
She will give you what you need
Leave those people that have greed
You have deeper missions Queen
Live your moments flying free

Warrior
You're my warrior

Node 5

Warriors Arrived
[next gen Queens and Kings]

~I'll take no Defeat!~

Dearest Warriors of the next gen; Queens and Kings,

May these words find you empowered. You may already know that the world is in dire need of YOUR wisdom and abilities. The sea levels are rising, the climate is unprecedentedly changing, the forests are vanishing and the humans are fighting. Former generations may not admit that YOU are of paramount importance to the entry of higher vibrations, unity, and a greener thriving world. Without your wisdom, humanity may be eradicated sooner than anticipated.

In your walk of life, you may experience misery, fear, anxiety, and negative thoughts. Although things may feel impossible with these emotional intensities, you have the ability to stop the projection of these emotions to your connected warrior network. Instilling fear in anyone will cause the stagnation of energy flow for both the fear-giver and receiver. May you recognize this if you sense this feeling within you. Fighting without purpose will exhaust your energy. Therefore, battle only for collective liberation. **Your peace of mind is the best vibe you can gift to anyone.** Of course, no one is happy, and peaceful all the time. Attaining peace is a trained thought. When you are tranquil with yourself, your vibration elevates. Mindfulness stretches your ability to solve problems, and generalizes it to the layers of possibilities. Mindfulness may take on a personal approach and tap into the higher senses. The ruling and serving warriors own resilience and unity. When the warrior network activates, the missions require the use of collaboration and unity. Competition does not exist within the chain of connections in the warrior network. This system is decentralized with personal power and creativity, in which political parties, governed minds, and control will be deemed superfluous. As a ruler and a servant to Nature, you exchange light by emanating Love and vibrating higher. The highest self is active through creation. Through creative ascension, you teach others about *Housing* their Earth suit for *Higher Consciousness.* At some point, everyone questions their existence and their mission on Earth, dear warrior. However, the sacred task of empowering your generation that is seeking answers and guidance, is an ongoing mission and endless task. So, how do you teach an entire generation to serve through selflessness? It is done through the practice of tranquility, which imparts knowledge. The chaos of the outer world blocks the receptors to the inner world. However, the practice of tranquility through meditation further ascends the self and overall awareness.

Earth's vibrations are calling you, Queens and Kings. The hunger for peace, equal opportunity, racial equality, end of poverty, and the appreciation of each other's religious differences, is deficient. Rules from past times are not applicable to this current demographic and ethnic fusion. Everything that is called into existence has an opposite. The opposite of peace is war. Love opposes hate and abundance opposes scarcity. Each opposing side needs to exist in order for one side to tilt and overtake for mass adaptation. The programming of greed and entitlement will lead a whole new generation to the path of hatred, which amplifies humanity's constraints. These constraints make you oblivious to the discovery of your conscious reality. The collective missions power your vibrations and steers your differences into empathy, while serving the whole network as a standalone node. This is clearly visible in freedom fighters who are standing in resistance. Their drive is to think innovatively to unlock enlightenment of the conscious mind. Hurting another living being, on any level, is strictly domination, and mind-control. You are the masters of your minds. When the mind commits to "join" organized entities and groups, it repels every other potential possibility. Millions of entities exist which create further division. Think about this division as it exists everywhere. This division also exists in scientific research when scientists counter each other's research outcomes. Surely, you know that science and the world are constantly evolving. We heavily rely on scientific and mathematical explanations. Can you think of ways in which numbers are used to instigate and cause conflict against each other? This results in selfish accomplishment and competition. Data is human-made. Your ability to shape an ascending civilization does not have mathematical or scientific attestation. Therefore, your power is grand and strong. It is ineffable!

You are learning from the world that surrounds you, beloved Warrior. You will find that life brings both joyous and sad moments. Joyous moments delivering hope will help you pave your path. As a warrior, there will also be numerous teaching moments about the devastation and the lessons, from havocs that ensued. There is wisdom in the lessons of both birth and death which are commemorations. The living body-soul represents growth, while the body-soul that is transitioning out of this realm represents finality and stagnation. What you see with your eyes and what moves in front of you is your reality. On the other hand, mortality is when someone is no longer in this reality. When someone you Love is no longer here, the reflection of life will take you on a pilgrimage through affliction. Affliction evolves at intervals within the gates of feelings. Many feelings including reminiscence, guilt, joy, disappointments, and anger complete the commemorative puzzle of coping with grief. This complete puzzle reinvents "you" to wholeness. There is no shortcut as it pertains to healing. Time heals when the heart expresses gratitude. It is fundamental that you understand the lessons of living in gratitude so you may strive for unity before leaving your Earth suit, Warrior.

Instead of a mindset focused on successes tied to titles, degrees, fame, and monetary gains to acquire abundance, your aim should be to walk impactful with exhilaration to service the Earth. **Abundance will find you.** Your focus should be on building a civilization where interconnectedness forms a whole for all living beings on the planet. Conscious vibrations and messages are the creative and highest self that roams the Earth in authentic and organic ways. The higher self powers a new world of artists and mindful bio-architects. Integration of Nature's model into the human-made distributed connections, benefits all living beings. Natural intelligence is success by default. Growth is not an optional phenomenon; it happens irrespectively. This world is diverse and complex and each human being travels under unique circumstances. The arguments and discussions that take place on Earth create more complexity, and amplify egos. Generations need healing from dogma, bigotry, and capitalism. A prosperous world cannot equally house religious conflict, racial prejudice, homelessness, and hunger. The mind-game of success and failure is static. It limits you, as the Warrior of the next gen, and prevents you from being accountable to holding the vibrations of a flourishing planet. Raising the vibrations in yourself elevates those around you and ignites a movement where all earthlings ascend. No human should hurt at the hand of their humankind in their quest for liberation. When you unlock this wisdom, your natural talents help to create the world around you. Financial liquids or assets do not provide peace in the hearts of loved ones when you exit your avatar. **Only your efforts, your Love, and the creation of a better sphere, while you are here, will bestow a piece of your heart and soul to those you leave behind.** Your raised vibration elevates world peace and sustainability for Mother Earth. Furthermore, it illuminates every human encounter. With this mindset of elevating planet Earth's vibration, no human feels purposeless. All souls harness gifts to unlock nodes and their unique creations come together. Every human uses talent, arts, creativity, and knowledge on an individual level which forms a distributed web of interconnectivity. This web is built on Love, trust, empathy, and support to flourish YOU. The Warriors Arrived: Next Gen Queens and Kings.

Enclosed with Love, Empathy, and Power to YOU!

R.N.K.

Warriors Arrived (next gen Queens and Kings)

Taking everything from the saturated King
Continue to spread light for the Love of thee

I will take control
They depend on me
I'm taking everything
From the saturated King
Continue to spread light
For the Love of thee
I will work for peace
I will walk for peace
I'll take the higher road
As I will talk this peace
Yes, I have arrived
I'll take no defeat

I'll take no defeat
Always on repeat
Never ever question
When I offer seats
Zero point field
Operating system
Dropped down to zero
Modified existence
This is where it started
Birth of Osiris
Understanding problems

Patching the virus
Resistance transformations
Will cause the hesitation
And slow down the growth
Of this life celebration

Yes

We won't fight your hate with despise
We won't leave children to die
And we'll give
We'll give more
We'll give everything we stand for
You can keep your rules
Those won't serve us anymore

Taking everything from the saturated King

I will take control
They depend on me
I'm taking everything
From the saturated King
Continue to spread light
For the Love of thee
I will work for peace
I will walk for peace
I'll take the higher road
As I will talk this peace
Yes, I have arrived

Warriors Arrived [next gen Queens and Kings]

I'll take no defeat

To all the Warriors Arrived
Next gen Queens and Kings
Take no defeat!

When you grow your mind
Yeah di thing you get fi know
Man dem rule the land
Dem a tek di power low
We guh rise above
Kick di man dem off dem chair
Power to di people
Ye di people dem wah care

Look at the time and tell me what you know
Just Following steps
Of war
You'll never know
The world starts from your eyesight
give meaning in what you say
Dodge the souls that suffocate
And take your energy away

Vibrate Higher

I will take control
They depend on me
I'm taking everything

From the saturated King
Continue to spread light
For the Love of thee
I will work for peace
I will walk for peace
I'll take the higher road
As I will talk this peace
Yes, I have arrived
I'll take no defeat

Node 6

World of Pulsation

~Roaming senses, count these blessings, all these lessons~

We've been dreaming layers deep into the Universe

Dreaming into the sacred geometry of the Earth

Dreaming through growth

Our skins change daily , Like the leaves on the trees

Surrender, Abundance is here

Seek nothing, Be one with everything

Surrender effortlessly

Ever-connected

Observe, Music of the Earth

Programming the self

Laugh, Cry

Traveling inner-dimensions

Outer layers form self-similarity patterns

Dreaming together into this World of Pulsation

$\mathcal{I}$**nner dimensions** are frequency activations that elevate every human being at some point in their existence. It sonically elevates the silence of infinite ether (space) to notice the layers and depth of the inner voice. The belief in magic and complete surrender to the higher self awakens gratitude with every breath. What would conversations entail if consciousness was humanity's highest value?

They would call for:

1. The molding of a civilization that practices selflessness without expecting karma and carrying the pain of surrounding souls.

2. Showing empathy and embracing differences.

3. Treating the opinions of others as plugins and understanding that these plugins are unique.

4. Connecting and tapping higher into the neural network and activating energies in its highest capacity for inventions to serve humans and nature simultaneously.

Conversations would focus on mastering, reading, and following the inner guide. There would be no Wars! After all, why would anyone fight? A fully activated inner and outer world amplifies the societal voice which trusts the soul voice to lead. **Take a deep breath, in and out. Gratitude resides here. This is the beginning of the journey through your inner dimensions.**

Love knows no boundaries. Roam the depths of the world and witness the miracle of roots growing decentralized, on their own. A headquarters for Love does not exist. Love experiences and elevates naturally by returning to and recharging the soul for guidance. The soul combines the power of empathy and Love. Civilizations are capable of elevating in their entirety. The ego hurts when brains do not think alike. Egos create separations.

Choose Love as a focal point for one moment. Let's build a loving imaginary village of today's world. In this village, all genders will come together representing each religion and culture in this world. Within these groups, every section of identifiers will be present. How large is this village? It is imperative to point out that there are over 4000 religions in the world that are also divided into subsets. There are also over 3800 distinct cultures in the world. This village is substantial. This village has already taken on omnipresence. Each person has unique talents and despite individual differences, the villagers help each other. If flooding overcomes this village one day, each person would lend a helping hand leading the next person to safety. No villager will float above the flood because of their gender, race, background, culture or religious affiliations. This village sows the seeds for an empathetic world. Everyone co-exists to make up its whole. When Love coalesces in all forms, it vibrates at a higher frequency.

Love knows no boundaries. It combines forces and overcomes the flooding of the village. Love is holding hands and understanding that the differences that exist in homes, streets, neighborhoods, towns, cities, states, countries, continents, and the collective world are gifts to the existence of the human experience. Love carries out sacred and collective tasks. Love understands that when the village floods, the inventors and unique plugins are activated. Neurons wire for inventions to serve each other collectively. This breakdown of gender, religion, culture, race, skin color, and identifiers would not matter. Survival would teach us that co-existence makes life more meaningful.

Let's all build a loving village in our lives. In this village, there will be earthlings. These earthlings will Love.

It may seem far-fetched to invite the world to unity and deploy Love as the primary thought process. Co-existence is free while ego and power have a price. However, through constant progression, humanity takes on the task to elevate human civilization. Earth-suits shed but continue to carry out elevating vibrations throughout multiple lifetimes. The world rotates and the experience of a whole new night and day creates space for improvement and ascending elevation. The world changes slowly and steadily, resembling the uncaptured processes of the plant which are not visible to the bare eyes. Problems are resolved only to awaken ten new issues. Perhaps it should be viewed as room for ten more possibilities in the depth layers. This could mean ten more activated unique plugins from ten individual soul prints. Co-existence invites more potential, inventions and unique mindsets, which is a dance of new vibrations not encountered before. Creating in the name of Love enhances the vibration to create selflessly for all. Living in the dark causes consciousness quandary. This disbelief in higher consciousness is the soul seeking the pulsation of the world. The growth of the plant feeds the mind-body-soul code. When the task is to carry out the *Housing* of *Higher Consciousness*, shadow work surfaces. Shadow work is healing individual trauma to elevate the self. Creation is also healing without ego, arrogance or a God-complex. Thoughts of the World's Pulsation are what souls need to leave behind a thriving, improved, and loving civilization.

This mindset does not give the spiritual being fame or fortune. The soul settles in to attract what the nodes unlock. It is a well-calculated effort that the soul has performed over many lifetimes. Through intentional vibrations and soul connections, the model of the loving village is created. There will be lost souls that work against Love due to trauma. However, this must be healed with empathy instead of battle. The existence of both sides collides for one side to dominate its presence. The existence of both sides generates swirling energy. Cosmic scolding is in charge of lost souls, and the existence of this scolding serves gratitude. The bonds of light-workers are meant to unite and become stronger. Spiritual awakening gifts the understanding that those with hatred in their hearts need Love. Their suffering should not be judged. Unlocking nodes teaches more about their agony and expands human empathy. Heaven and hell are both in this lifetime, but the soul dreams into the Earth. Souls that carry hatred may travel through the darkness of the planet and live in a nightmare for thousands of years without awakening. Therefore, awaken into the dreaming of the Earth. By becoming light-workers to the soul journey of conscious vibrations, the Earth may dream light and elevation into this **World of Pulsation.**

World of Pulsation

I dream
I dream
Dream awake
Streaks of colored soft vibrations
Come with me
My hearts veins connected to the genesis
Soft-spoken heart is my longing.
Sharing starts belonging
My heart not ready
So it beats far too steady
Can I be here giving it already
To my own Love and vibration
Take me slow
Take me slow into
This World of Pulsation

No aggravation
Spirit sensation
Earthly relation
Self-domination
Controlling my mind
With my conscious vibration
No, I will not hype the world altercation
Reaching for souls seeking Love for hydration
I want that Love for its self-proclamation
Love it's this Love
In this World of Pulsation

This heart on overflow
I'm Minutes on-the-go
These Magic plants they know
Cortex warming glow
Feel this color show
Climax coming slow
I am in the clouds to flow
My inner self she knows
That messages occur
I focus in the realm
Would never play the plant
Or I will live the blur

Vibrate Higher
Into this
World of Pulsation

No aggravation
Spirit sensation
Earthly relation
Self-domination
Controlling my mind
With my conscious vibration
No, I will not hype the world altercation
Reaching for souls seeking Love for hydration
I want that Love for its self-proclamation
Love it's this Love
In this World of Pulsation

Silence your mind
Let me help you find her

Roaming senses
Count these blessings
All these lessons
Neurons eager
Voice and reason
Learning breathing
I can hear them
Language sparing
Inner caring
Yes, they know me
Yes, they hear me
Yes, they feel me

Close your eyes
Feel the vibrations
Focus
Vibrate
Vibrate Higher

No aggravation
Spirit sensation
Earthly relation
Self-domination
Controlling my mind
With my conscious vibration
No, I will not hype the world altercation

Reaching for souls seeking Love for hydration
I want that Love for its self-proclamation
Love it's this Love
In this World of Pulsation

Giving up my stress
Giving up my pain
Giving up the war
To the neurons in my brain
Giving up Consumption
That will bring my body low
Wired for expanding
To the things I need to know
Cause the things I need to know
Are the things I need to do
This is lifework for the world
It surpasses me and you
For the things that we claim their truth
And the opposites a lie
And the only truth that lives
Is the sure thing that we die

No aggravation
Spirit sensation
Earthly relation
Self-domination
Controlling my mind
With my conscious vibration
No, I will not hype the world altercation

Reaching for souls seeking Love for hydration
I want that Love for its self-proclamation
Love it's this Love
In this World of Pulsation

Ten billion neurons
Ten thou connections
Ancient Egyptians
Used 360 senses
Guidance and blessings
I've traveled dimensions
To sprinkle the world
With these nature life lessons
The Earth is our Mother
We need to stop trashing
She will overflow lava
And waves are crashing
Impending our caring
She will cure the masses
We owe it to her
We're alive through our clashes

Vibrate Higher

No aggravation
Spirit sensation
Earthly relation
Self-domination
Controlling my mind

With my conscious vibration
No, I will not hype the world altercation
Reaching for souls seeking Love for hydration
I want that Love for its self-proclamation
Love it's this Love
In this World of Pulsation

Node 7

Matriarchy Rising

~The Matriarchy is here, and we're not going anywhere~

Get ready for the unexpected. Get ready for transformation.

The Matriarchy is actively participating in ascending the human vibrations by showing up in a multitude of forms. The stories are exhibited in thousands of avatars with deep wounded narratives awakening empathy. This movement is a manifested experience. When the Matriarchy is ready to manifest, the power unifies. **Get ready to experience your magic beyond this point. You are now powered by the Matriarchy Rising.**

Mother is powered by the Universe to house life, unify, provide health, and instill knowledge through the Earth and its magic. The feminine principle is viewed as "weak". Yet, this forms and carries life. No institution nurtures the menstrual cycle and honors the woman's body. The Divine menstruating body requires rooted understanding from a moving civilization. All the while, the body on a cycle also requires respite.

Matriarchy is not the opposite of Patriarchy. Patriarchy resides within the Matriarchy. This is realized through Mothers that housed the human when DMT was first released within bodies for the very first time, close to birth. Mothers are the collective deities to the energy field of the Earth. Mothers carry some of Earth's heaviest tasks for solidarity. They often get overlooked and their collective power can light up the Earth and will reveal a stronger, more inclusive world. Mothers have wisdom, which cannot be understood with rationality, but awakens through the magic and eternity of their souls. This phenomenon encapsulates the wisdom of the Universe. The wisdom, transcended by the Matriarchy, is the "Mothers of the World", the sacred womb of life, and the undeniable nurture which comes from a thicker source than blood. Mother is Nature. Mother is Earth. Mother is the energy of one's Mother or the person in whom "Mother" energy is found. Mother, the Divine, has helped to understand that Love, peace, race, religion, and genders are not exclusions, but the sources that beam equal light. "Mother" has an avatar on Earth that will accept and battle lower vibrations for the sake of humanity. Mother comes in a multitude of forms. The Matriarchy Rising is the Mother for all of humanity in elevation, with no exclusions.

Nurturing is needed along the edges of basic humanity. It starts with Nature and works inwards towards humans. **Position yourself in the Universe and from this angle, zoom in. When zooming in, you will see the seas and continents clearer. Zoom in closer and you will find Nature, mountains, and tall trees. Zoom in further to see animals and landscape. Then, with a significantly more advanced zoom, we encounter Humans.** Humans that:

1. Place flags on Earth and claim land.

2. Engineer weapons for war and fight to dominate each other.

3. Rape, murder, steal, and hurt their own species.

4. Hunt, hurt, and breed other species for the overconsumption of food, trophies, entertainment and proclaim absolute truth, using their hatred.

Although this perspective on reality seems dire, there are other outlooks. These outlooks can elevate humanity. Fortunately, there is light in humanity and this effulgence is used to ignite the flame of Empathy and Love.

The microcosm ultimately experiences the entire Universe within itself. Imagine the majority of people connecting to each other through the microcosm. The world's nurturing leaders will operate from the most inner layer and work their way to the outer layers. This sacred task is divine elevation practiced through the self for the collective missions. The Matriarchal consciousness provides the solutions to all of the "problems" in the world. It nurtures the canopies of the forest to the roots of Nature's veins and spreads light through the network. Matriarchal consciousness knows and operates from this wisdom. It seeks guidance from the waterfalls, seasonal leaves, and understands why the beehive is fundamental to existence. The Matriarchy is powered by Gaia, breathing as one. The Matriarchy is guided by Nature's law which inhales and exhales through Gaia's Divine gifts.

Humanity implements regulatory laws for animals, plants, and themselves. As time progresses it is unearthed that these rules are structured to hold the freedom of earthlings hostage. What is this powerful energy which fuels the Matriarchy and scares the patriarchal consciousness? Is the suppression of the Matriarchal consciousness, over hundreds of years, caused by the incredible power it harnesses? The Matriarchy is magic. It is magic gifted in the forms of creation. It is an effortless creation. The feminine principle ejects itself from dogma and taps into the higher forms of existence. The Matriarchy understands that human experiences introduce countless layers of possibilities. This consciousness understands that life does not house limitations. Altered states, explorations, and inventions are the gifts of Higher Consciousness.

Time is cyclical. Human Nature has cycled through times such as prehistoric, ancient, ice-age, volcanic eruptions, and tectonic shifts which birthed new lands. Human civilizations were wiped out and it will happen again. It is the cycle of Nature and time. Will human engineering, their writings, and tangible creations survive? Although it is questionable whether tangible creations will make it into the "future", Souls will cycle through lifetimes and are eternal. Through rituals, plant medicine, art, and cosmic magic, human nature is remembered. Ancestral trauma is healed through the dances and performance of healing rituals with the use of plant medicine. For thousands of years, humans have roamed the Earth and through guidance from nature, enlighten the planet. Gaia is Mother, and humanity learns from her. **Listen, and be guided through Mother Gaia.**

The Rising Matriarchy is a soul-vibration which falls deeply into the layers of conscious awakening. Through individualism for the collective, Love, ancient teachings, spoken words, writing, art, music, dance, and magic honor the Divine. The breath is gifted through the Divine. Collectively breathing and healing sets off a chain effect of Higher Vibration. There is no shame in development as it shapes the human that it has become. Through healing, energy transcends strength and power to the avatars that suffer the mindset of irreparable trauma. Collective individuality is the "Universal brain" and the different minds that make up the whole. Thinking alike still sets humans apart. Differing opinions should not source problems but invite open-source possibilities and new pathways to create and relate. The images that the eyes take in are processed in the brain and then outputted in the form of knowledge. Storing different information through fundamental points of view teaches Empathy.

The Rising Matriarchy understands that when limitations are created there is a critical need for expansion. Limitations are superfluous. Limiting thoughts or behaviors create the opposite of those thoughts and behaviors which automatically surface and seek growth. When a line is drawn in endeavors, curiosity seeks the other side of that line. This may take one generation, or five, but curiosity and unity will diminish borders. There is only one Earth. It is a birthright to move around freely, as all human beings are gravitated to this planet, with their feet, to roam in all directions. This world serves collectively. The Matriarchy raises generations that will service the Earth and do right by **Mother**. The air that will be breathed is sacred and clean. Pure growth of green lands is the mission of the Matriarchy. Homes become sustainable when the Matriarchy raises the human vibration. Nothing can stop the Matriarchy from Rising. Domination plays as the Matriarchy moves in sensible ways.

Male servers of the Matriarchy understand that life gifts through the sacred womb. Acceptance of the female and male principle bears spiritual children that become future leaders. The future leaders nurture the Earth and the World. The Matriarchy powers all existence and is neutral to the sexes, as all forms of earthlings belong to the human race. **The rise of the Matriarchy is both the awakened female and awakened male in non-duality.** Some will still need to awaken to the truth of their Nature and travel through cosmic scolding to encounter all of existence, in every life-form. Everything that is here, in this world that co-exists today, is Nature. Although pushed away by the laws, rules, and unswerving belief of personal conviction, **humankind belongs to Nature**. When a soul feels trapped in an avatar, it will seek change. Also, this change is Nature taking on another human experience. Resistance to this will not make it less Godly. Nature is the Divine providing the **Breath of Life**. Acceptance elevates the Matriarchy to walk every human through all the strengthening and falling layers of human vibrations, to a higher frequency. Wherever there is Love to welcome all Loving and empathetic walks of life, the Matriarchy is Rising. The Matriarchy Rising leads by holding the royal torch of endless light. The Matriarchy is here to stay!

Matriarchy Rising

We have turned this world
Into your home
Wait until we come into our own
We are marching
For the things they've claimed
Wait until we start
The royal flame

Start to spread the flame
Our royal torch of endless light
Our understanding network support
That's controlled at night
Where Love makes rights
And leverage everything
That Queens are owed
Yes, she's a CEO
Independently she codes
Creating this whole world
Where she has more human time
That nurtures once a month
Before she gives you her nine
These Bodies carry young ones
We can take that endless pain
And yes, you compliment us
But we're wisdom in the game

Wisdom in the game

Sagacious with our plans
When raising youngs by themselves
Queens prove that again
And the social system might just favor
Adam and commands
Check back in with us
When we rule economies and lands
We have planned to give it all
Nurturing the Earth from roots
And if you want to dominate
You can join our lady troops
We will hire all the macho, Sexist speakers
That we've known
Killing every vibe of ours
Where we mandatory glow

Mandatory glow
You already know
Women running things
That scares you
We already know
We're just working low-key
Watching domination play
We're never worried as the truth is
What we will convey
Plus, we don't care that you don't
Want us leading with our core
We have Intelligence
To break down your

Matriarchy Rising

Attenuated door
Don't take this as a threat

We are leading with the free
These are verses to the
Scripture of our Matriarchy

We have turned this world
Into your home
Wait until we come into our own
We are marching
For the things they've claimed
Wait until we start
The royal flame

Node 8

Binary Human

~It's time to look up, your zeros and ones need some leveling up~

$\mathcal{M}$oney is a resource created by mankind. Before this resource was recognized, humans were traders of services. This meant that one person exchanged their talent or specialty with another person, for their strong suit. Services were also traded for crops or livestock. As mankind ventured by exploring the world, new paradigms were introduced. The paradigms of a universal exchange started with a few Earth elements. Gold and silver became the touchstone for coins. The exchange of the coins has a value derived from a meeting of the minds. The coin is neither the service nor the final investment. It is the exchange for services and commodities. Unbeknownst to an ego-less and moneyless world, human civilization voyages the Earth through ether and battles over the exchange of resources. Collective tasks are the "well" for human prosperity. Without the well, there is no access to water. Humankind requires a shift in mentation to

77

impel water. Water, a free resource from the Divine, is sustenance to Earth's inhabitants. Yet, no one can drink from the well. The well is surrounded by barbed wire and guarded in rotation by self-proclaimed "guards of the well". The well is only accessible with the exchange of money. Humankind, summoned by "human nature", adapted plant medicine. The body, a natural healing system in collaboration with Nature, has reset functions. Yet, humankind receives care through the exchange of "health insurance". The body's illness is in rotation by a self-proclaimed country and its "healthcare system". Moreover, foods of the Earth provide nutrition and healing. Similarly, they are guarded in rotation by organic and anomalous processed foods. The freedom to choose unnatural is "chewing and swallowing" the barbed wire which surrounds the "guards of the well". Organic choices should be by default. When the Earth gifts nutrition, it is manipulated by the guards. Earth heals and has built-in ways to protect itself. In this regard, when organic is not honored, organic will become invasive in order to survive.

Humankind operates on nodes. The healer, nurturer, builder, and inventor all live within. Humanity knows exactly how to serve the Earth and each other through understanding the survival of species. Throughout Nature's network, nodes operate for the collective. In many ways, humans provide

Binary Human

this service to Earth, but most people greed the increased monetary exchange for more material gains. Throughout Gaia's distributed web, the incredible network of nature is witnessed. An abundance of species reside and operate daily in the decentralized ecosystem. Bees, for instance, are highly decentralized. They work collectively in the beehive. Their understanding of serving the beehive comes through their bee tasks. For instance, worker bees naturally know their job and use swarm intelligence to protect their hive and Queen Bee. Bees do not wonder about their bee lifespan. Each bee serves its ecosystem through natural ability. The bees run a healthcare system that identifies bees with ill health, guides them out of the hive, diagnoses them, and nurtures them back to health. This is the Ayurvedic bee doctor working with Nature's plant intelligence. This collective intelligence detects when something is wrong within the beehive network. There is no guard mentality or exchange involved. They are operating from their decentralized and ever-connected nodes. Through these nodes, they activate with empathy for each other. The goal is collective and collaborative survival. Bees pollinate and contribute to the production of the fruits and vegetables which humans consume. Bees are important to our well-being, and to emphasize this, they serve our existence. Without our bees, our colorful landscape would not exist and humans would not survive. They are the architects of flower abundance.

79

Humankind takes Mother Nature's engineers for granted. Harmful pesticides and fertilizers do not allow our beloved bees to pollinate. When bees decrease in population, humans are in danger. Growing organic naturally allows bees to thrive. It provides a cleaner, healthier, and nutritious realm.

Organic choices are by default. Options are unwarranted. Natural fertilizers and pesticides are defaults. The worship of attaining money and "guards of power" kill our ecosystem. Through draconic indoctrination, human civilization voyages the Earth through ether, and battles over the exchange of resources.

Welcome a world with honor and respect to Gaia and her resources. With a decentralized effort, humankind may live in a world employed by the Earth. In this elevated vibration, power and money are devoid. Serving the Earth, and its higher vibrational inhabitants, benefits all of humankind. Exploiting the Earth for its resources is dishonorable and despicable. Ingratitude is a pandemic. Greed for power and money are chronic viruses. Collective intelligence is caring for the land, growing foods, and learning the gift of plant medicine. The celebration of humankind, as spiritual beings, is an elevated, advanced, and magical human experience.

The spiritual brain Vibrates Higher.

Finances cannot provide natural resources. Monetary greed destroys the ecosystem. Polluted air stifles breathing. Oxygen is sacred and precious. Humankind learns when oxygen becomes a commodity. All the possibilities in life are guarded on the outside and inside layers. Education, Love, gender, religion, and authority stand guards in the layers. The layers have rules that connect to guidelines. It is a Human birthright to challenge everything. Possibilities in life poison the guards.

Be free, Love, and honor the possibilities of endless branches connecting to your peace of mind. Having a mind of your own will be met with resistance. Step out of the normalized chase of "things".

When you enter the realm, you need to let go of the things that you know, learn, and believe.

Binary Human

Money
Honey

Tell me
Can you breathe this money?
If you killed the makers
Of this magic golden honey?
Can you plant this money
Earthly science
Make it grow?
If this is a no
Decentralize
Power dies
We're moving slow
Bam!

Baffled by your rules
And I don't like em.'
Devils tell me
People like me
Are not likened
I don't really care
I just have a message
Vibrating you to 360 senses

Binary human,
It's time to lookup

Your zeros and ones
Need some leveling up
And this is the time to
Believe in yourself
When your Third Eye connects
I need you to trust in yourself

When you enter the realm
You need to let go of the things
That you know and learned and believe
And the timing is perfect
The Earth she will call
Patterns will form
Vision will stall
To the mind and the beauty of things
The trees they will breathe
Earthly rings
You're an empath
You'll see
Moving with me
Through the chants of the forest
They will set you free

You will learn to be free
360 degrees

Baffled by your rules
And I don't like em'
Devils tell me

People like me
Are not likened
I don't really care
I just have a message
Vibrating you to 360 senses
Tell me
Can you breathe this money?
If you killed the makers
Of this magic golden honey?
Can you plant this money
Earthly science
Make it grow?
If this is a no
Decentralize
Power dies
We're moving slow
Bam!

Money
Honey

Node 9

Inner Compass

~My soul voice is speaking to anyone close, but I'm reaching for far~

Ancient Egyptians had a funerary book called, **The Book of the Dead**. The Book of the Dead, an artistic cryptic scroll, imparted guidance, magic spells, and formulae for individuals traveling to the afterlife, which is referred to as "A'Aru". The book reflects the individual's life lived on Earth which was drawn as hieroglyphs and repeated on the walls of the deceased's tomb. The customary assembly of hieroglyphs was committed to papyrus. Each life story ended with facing Osiris, the deity of the dead. There are numerous ancient stories of Osiris including the murder of Osiris by his envious brother, Seth, for his position on the throne. Osiris's body was dismembered and scattered over twenty-six locations and was sought by his mourning wife, Isis. Isis had magical powers and used these powers to briefly bring back Osiris to life to conceive and witness the birth of their child, Horus. Osiris went on becoming God of the Underworld.

Osiris had responsibilities, including weighing the heart of the deceased against the feather of an ostrich for equilibrium. The ostrich feather represented Ma'at, the Goddess of truth, justice, and cosmic balance. The scale was scrutinized by the deity, Anubis, and its outcome was recorded by the deity, Thoth (also referred to as Tehuti). If the heart of the deceased and the feather were balanced on the scale, Osiris would grant eternal life for the sacred realm, to the soul of the deceased. If the heart of the deceased outweighed the feather, it meant the soul would travel the Netherworld. The journey going into and through the Netherworld is also referred to as "The Field of Reeds". The Netherworld, the "cosmic scolding" journey, is unique to the dead. Therefore, each assemblage across items and scrolls was authentic in its spells, guidance, and prayers. Information about the phenomenal ancient earthlings of Egypt, once Kemet, is mostly guessed from the lost translation of hieroglyphs. The ancient Egyptians were rich in otherworldly innovations and advanced technology. They understood the use of energy, the spirals of life, and sacred geometry. Perfectly preserved embalmed bodies in the sarcophagus, within tombs, conserved some of the most ancient and mystical revelations. Their incredibly advanced civilization provoked speculations about the usage of ancient Egypt's innovations and how these innovations contribute to current civilization. Kemet's people used 360 senses. Cosmically connected, this ancient civilization experienced 360 senses in their sensory modulation. They understood that their pineal gland activates the microcosm. Their in-tune feminine principle was honored through magic, art, and spell casting. It kept most of this ancient civilization highly intrigued with the magic of the soul, death, and the afterlife. Their belief honors the dead in sacred vibration. What if the excavation of their ancient tombs moves the energy field of the encapsulated higher frequencies and higher states of consciousness? The Giza plateau, which perfectly positioned the Giza pyramids to the Orion Belt constellation, is said to form a magnetic energy field. Could it be that negative vibrations awaken when artifacts are moved from their energy field? **May this passage awaken your consciousness.** Ancient Egyptians used 360 senses. To truly understand 360 senses, look beyond the possible and it will eventually introduce endless possibilities. Magic through the spiritual body unlocks neurons and surrenders to higher states. When it is realized that the brain is a field that locks and unlocks neurons, it is understood that all Universal information resides within the human vessel. Thenceforth, nodes unlock the microcosm.

The Inner Compass guides. Stress, fear, fatigue and anger weaken the connection to the internal compass frequency that guides the human experience. This results in clouded perception. The spiritual mind weakens in signal strength. Thus, it works harder to wire the patterns of courage and empathy, which are all connected to the primordial state. It further triggers a domino effect to which the physical body reacts and a series of internal events take place. Furthermore, the flow of energy stagnates which leads to a weakened immune system and organ issues. The Inner Compass cannot successfully connect when anxiety is present. A successful connection requires surrender. Awareness through mindful breathing calms anxiety levels. The human experience, as a standalone node, ultimately understands that the authentic journey of the human experience is calm. Through constant awareness, the Inner Compass activates, and anxiety vanishes. At every moment, the self is responsible for declaring and manifesting the state of self-awareness. The standalone node is aware and mindful. When the Earth suit dies, it becomes one with the cyclic Earth, the primordial spirals. The Soul, however, declares no arrival or departure. **Immortal, unassailed and ineffable, the Soul is ever constant with the Universe.**

Housing Higher Consciousness is not a chase. It does not belong to any industry. *Housing Higher Consciousness* cannot become a capitalistic endeavor since the spiritual bank does not know finances. Humans that lack self-belief and trust are more apt to relinquish power to those "selling" ancient teachings. All the while, every human being is capable of *Housing* their *Higher Consciousness* through self-awareness, practice, and stillness. Ancient teachings are gifted over many lifetimes. Conscious wealth accumulates through the self. Cosmic vibration powers the creation of sacred work. Cosmic vibrations and conscious wealth uphold the natural ability to walk through cosmic interference. Cosmic interference is not an easy or beautiful phenomenon. The interference finds the depth of ancestral, parental, and individual trauma. There is no shortcut. Silence the self. The neural network of receptors needs practice for activation. **Take care of the body temple. It is where you reside. It is your place of worship.** The Divine is worshiped from within. Through self-love, the Divine is honored. Fueling the body with Earth's nutrition allows the Inner Compass to guide. Commit to the practice to activate the Inner Compass. The compass creates new patterns and space for possibilities. Observe and awaken the World. Lower vibrational self-talk complicates the awakening process. Anxiety and stress are observed and forget the Higher Conscious state. Bearing the weight of other travelers, through their human experience, is diminished when meditation is practiced. When the avatar Houses Higher Consciousness, the weight is no longer heavy. With the absence of the heaviness, the spiritual body is driving in full motion to master Love. The spiritual body does not accept less than magnificent Love. Love spirals and pulls from deeper healing energy that is sourced in the spiritual body. The Inner Compass trusts itself. The guidance of the Inner Compass regards "others" as "self" in their human experience.

Lighting gateways connect in the same manner that celestial bodies connect through dark matter. Polarizing opposites create more substantial networks. The nodes that connect to the good vibrations create positive energy. Whereas, the nodes that connect to the bad vibrations create negative energy. Higher and lower vibrations accumulate "pulse connections" and "set intentions". Positive collective intentions vibrate primordial patterns, while selfish choices ignite our ego and augment the inner and outer struggle. The awakening of the world is achieved when it is practiced and when humanity activates its Inner Compass. Beams of light of the Inner Compass traverse the Globe. The mission of awakening encompasses all avatars and walks of life. The Soul is the unconcealed truth of the ever-connected Inner Compass, which repeats the patterns of the primordial state. The *Inner Compass,* however infinitesimal, is *the compass of life* and the *inner dimension your eye needs to see.*

Inner Compass

Trust that you know what you do
Give it your guidance and truce
Trust that the roots of the light that you bring
Is connected through eye of Horus

The book of the dead
We've not held in exalt
Given it disregard
My soul voice is speaking
To anyone close
But I'm reaching for far
The Giza plateau needs its treasures
That was stolen from their rightful location
Without it
We cannot unlock the messages
Through the highest civilization

Rulers of the skies
Don't make me fall from Grace
Shiva sounding drums
Still saving human race
Crisis of our consciousness
Has left them insecure
7 billion humans trapped within the made-up blur
Yet the inner compass guidance
Sends us back to peace
Watch confessions made

Just to lay and rest in peace

Trust that you know what you do
Give it your guidance and truce
Trust that the roots of the light that you bring
Is connected through eye of Horus

Housing Higher Consciousness
Through everything we know
Without wording from the past
Love will never grow
Yet the inner compass
Is ignored through all this fear
Hurting animals
Through their hunting
And their scare
I am here to stand up for our peace
And what it's worth
For the people dragged through dirt
While they're hungry and they're hurt
And for everyone that dares to say
That I am absurd
Cosmic scolding is the judge
To your final words
Tehuti is magic
Through writing my spells
Thousands of years ago
Through conscious wealth
Vibrating higher

Through Orion's Belt
Climate is judged
By the things that they melt
Logic is that what we burn will go up
Must come down
And this will settle in dust
This is the chemicals rooted in Earth
Killing our Eco and poisoning dirt

A ka dua
Tuf ur biu
Bi a'a chefu
Dudu nur af an nuteru

The book of the dead
We've not held in exalt
Given it disregard
My soul voice is speaking
To anyone close
But I'm reaching for far
I'm reaching for you
Through my light
And my soul
And dimensions I've seen
The compass of life
Is the inner dimension
Your eye needs to see

Node 10

Dharma (practice)

~Sit down in Peace, let your Third Eye increase~

Celebrations are a common practice when an infant enters this world. Where does the soul live before it enters the birth canal? Humanity understands that a human body is created in the Mother's womb. Death, however, is not commonly celebrated. The dead are mourned. Emotional upheavals of loss, sadness, anger, and fear accompany the grieving stages which can cloud reality. What will happen now? Pain may feel unbearable at times. Death is all around. Death is a circulation of incoming and outgoing energy every moment, of every day. At this very moment, as you read this, life is surrounded by death. Plants, insects, animals, humans, and all living entities are born to die. It is the passage through the incoming and outgoing portals of the cosmos. Souls are released while the physical form goes back into the Earth. Although this may be the reality of avatars, it is still hard to understand that death makes a full circle of life.

There has never been a witness that has returned in their physical form to recount their after-death scenarios. It is a mystery. Dreaming into the imaginal realm unlocks ways to understand temporary bodies and soul travel. However, souls upgrade and downgrade according to the life it has lived. Death is an integral part of life. Killing for sport or recreation is not a natural phenomenon. It is not natural to hurt animals or invade Gaia and her species, including humans, as this will affect the planet's vibration. Immoral killings cycle a stagnant vibrational state. Poachers and murderers will eventually understand that the price is vibrational cosmic scolding. There is no explanation for how scolding works. Each individual walks through this on their own. Hunting for survival has a fundamentally different vibration than killing for amusement. May earthlings understand the difference before manifesting their vibrational cosmic scolding.

Dharma is cosmic law connected through the network of Gaia and all earthlings. Humans do not oversee this law. It is unwritten and plays out into life on Earth. When humans break cosmic rules, in addition to vibrational change, the brain nodes alter and there is always a unique form of consequence. Whether one reaches the ending days of their lives, and sentence has not yet prevailed, cosmic scolding takes retribution far beyond life on Earth. Body networks run through the bottom of feet and the palms of hands which parallels the roots of trees and the veins of animals, plants, and fungi. This connects every life form on Earth which spirals into the cosmos. However, this may seem foreign when human perception is clouded. The neural network resembles the roots and veins that run throughout the world. Dharma is the state of remembrance. **Refrain from seeking or acquiring Dharma; practice stillness.** Opening up the spiritual gateways to elevate to Dharma is a constant manifestation of the mind. **Practice silence and mindfulness to raise the vibration surrounding planet Earth.** The mind understands the practice mode to respect all life and death. This very moment is unique. No thoughts are required when falling layers deep within the self. Breathing happens effortlessly, which is a natural phenomenon. Beliefs, however, take possession which make silence a task to accomplish. Through practicing and learning, meditation will no longer be a strive, but a reality. **Do not give up. Try again tomorrow.** Dharma is already here, awaiting your Divine presence. Choosing the self is the most selfless act. Self-love and self-care comes before Love and care for others. This might be perceived as being selfish. **Love the self, regardless.** Listen to the missions in life. Lifework is vibrated to Dharma for collective liberation. The path traveled is journeyed as a standalone node. There is non-duality between humans and nature. Humans can operate on their own without the need for another human to carry out their life mission. Thousands of years ago, the ancestry of humans have walked down the Dharmic path, transcending their wisdom. Deep down, the heart understands this wisdom. Although it is hard to explain Dharma's definition, it plays the melody of the spiritual mind, body, and soul in harmony. **Dharma is the soul code. Vibrate higher to the state.**

Dharma to the fullest. Dharma for oneself.

Dharma (practice)

36,000 years ago
I gave you everything you needed to know
Now you question; why?
Why am I here?
Am I gonna die?
Don't let me live in that fear

In order to protect them all
Let us state the truth
We don't need to hunt the leopard
Evil has a root
Many times they're cowards
Watch them travel in a group
No one needs a tusk
But keep invading nature with your troops
Evil eyes
Are based inside the earthlings
Watch them do the evil
While they're smirking
Like they are protected
From vibrational scolding
There is ease in compassion
And enlightened worldlings
Cosmic order spreading
Flirtatious wording
Spread it for yourself and no one else
Dharma to the fullest

Dharma for oneself
Engraved in the palm of your hand
It is nature's networks
Running all throughout the lands
We are here situated
With this brilliant mind
Don't get robbed from your moments
And the things that are sublime
By the sense of time

By the sense of time

36,000 years ago
I gave you everything you needed to know
Now you question; why?
Why am I here?
Am I gonna die?
Don't let me live in that fear

Sit down in peace
Let your Third Eye increase
The Programming starts
When your thoughts are released
Fairly Give yourself time
Time to practice and learn
And you will shed some people
Some people will turn
To the left and the right
And you need to choose you
You cannot grow yourself

Dharma (practice)

Without watering you
And some people will feel
Like their energies' out
That will be the sign
That you will need to tap out

And you will feel detached
Because you will be detached
But your calling
Is calling your soul-print to match

You won't be alone
You will travel home
Plugged into the plants
Guided through the realm
You'll be singled out
Cosmic order route
Missions to fulfill
Now it starts the thrill
Life will give you everything
Euphoria will spill
Dharma to the fullest
Dharma for oneself

36,000 years ago
I gave you everything you needed to know
Now you question; why?
Why am I here?
Am I gonna die?
Don't let me live in that fear

Dharma (practice)

Node 11

Vibrate Higher

~Vibrate Higher, light within~

$\mathcal{R}$eleasing things that do not serve life allows Higher Vibration to multiply. The vibration further recognizes necessities over luxury and frees the mind from self-limitations, and people-worship. New and conscious patterns diligently create strengthened wiring. Endless spirals are the pathways to Higher Vibrations. **Take time and nurture the soul, as it has gone through thousands of years of energy gateways, and replenished nodes.** There are no "Highest" Vibrations, only "Higher" Vibrations.

Ayurveda is an over 5000-year-old natural, medicinal system that originated in India. It is a system with a deep-rooted understanding of mind-body-soul programs. It has various activation points such as Chakras, Nadis and glands which connect energy through the body and channel it throughout the system. In Sanskrit, "Cakra" (Chakras) are wheels and "Nāḍī" (Nadis) are the channels. Ayurveda counts 72,000 Nadis (nanoscopic Chakras) in the body, with the three main Nadis being the Sushumna, Pingala, and Ida. The Sushumna Nadi runs alongside the 7 Chakras through the middle of the spine. Pingala and Ida swirl up the Sushumna channel, while flowing in and out of the 7 Chakras. Pingala and Ida are also commonly referenced as Shiva (masculine principle) and Shakti (feminine principle) and Shiv-Shakti in harmonious union. Pingala Nadi is breathing through the right nostril. This activates the left side of the brain and body, which connects to the solar-outward looking Shiva, the masculine principle. Ida Nadi is breathing through the left nostril. This activates the right side of the brain and body, which connects to the lunar-inward looking Shakti, the feminine principle. The masculine and feminine principles have nothing to do with the characteristics of the male and female genders, as we know them. Feminine and masculine principles refer to the body's Ayurvedic composition. It is fundamental to understand that each human has a unique Ayurvedic composition. Energy, referred to as Prana, can travel within the body in 72,000 directions. Ether, referred to as Akasha, is found throughout the body maintaining its Akashic records. The Akashic records encode the entire existence of the macrocosm into the microcosm. Prana and Akasha, always in coexistence, can be visualized as "Energy dancing in Ether". The first of the seven prominent Chakras is at the root of the spine, and the last one is at the crown. The Chakras swirl up as the metaphoric serpent. Each Chakra is classified by various attributes. Amongst these attributes are Elements, Names (Sanskrit), Plexus, Lotus petal count, Hindu Deity association, and Mantra activation. The Chakras harness deep relations to energetic flow, disorders, and connections to the physiological system.

The 7 Chakras

Element	Name	Plexus	Petals	Deity	Mantra
Earth	Muladhara	Root	4	Ganesha	Lam
Water	Svadhishthana	Sacral	6	Brahma	Vam
Fire	Manipura	Solar	10	Vishnu	Ram
Air	Anahata	Heart	12	Rudra	Yam
Ether	Vishuddhi	Throat	16	Jivatma	Ham
Light	Ajna	Third Eye	2	Paramatmaa	Sam ksham
Bliss	Sahasrara	Crown	1000	Sadashiva	Aum

When aligned, these seven Chakras awaken the main energy channels. Starting with the serpent energy, coiled at the spine's base, the swirling **Muladhara's** four petals connect to emotions of self-confidence, security, and body image. The serpent's life moves through Nadis to penetrate each Chakra with focus, and practice. Both the yin and yang energy are called into existence to surface. Emotions that are surfaced by **Muladhara** give control over the self to observe emotions with stillness. Observing the self with deeper trust and surrender, shakes insecurities. **Muladhara** opens up with greater ease with the silence of the mind.

The serpent ascends moving through **Svadhishthana's** six "petaled" "wheel". It surfaces liveliness, creativity, vexation, and the ultimate harmony of gender identity. Observe the previously opened channel of emotions from **Muladhara**. It holds vigor to **Svadhishthana.**

Once a Chakra is powered, it feeds fundamental wisdom to the next. Open channels power creativity and light whereby blocked channels harbor vexation and weigh a heavy heart.

Trusting in the serpent's travel through **Manipura's** fiery ten "petals", opens gateways to intimacy. This Chakra will magnify reputation, fear, and anxiety. **The opening of Manipura gives a broader sense of peace collected over the practice of Muladhara and Svadhishtana. It harnesses understanding of the Earth and Water elements, as it pertains to Fire.**

Vibrate Higher

Fire needs an Earth element to burn and a Water element to extinguish. The element of Fire burns what does not serve but provides for what does serve.

The serpent swivels through the twelve "petaled" "air wheel" to provide its feathery energy. This resolves feelings collected throughout the Chakra swirl which activates the next Chakra, **Anahata.** Here, emotional pain may still surface but gives in-depth observation and self-awareness. Healing and release will come in waves of emotions and serve as therapy for a lifetime. Allowing this energy to flourish, offers longevity to the redirection of emotions that surface.

Ether's infinite expanse, controlled by the serpent's gyration through sixteen "petals", enters the throat and unleashes expression. Base alignment of this **Vishudhhi** Chakra invokes energy in the back of the neck propelling emotions of integrity and self-trust. It echoes a more incredible feeling of control and the alignment of the avatar to the spiritual body. Joy is the given emotion through **Vishudhhi.** Emotional work is done for the self, and not for the ego or control.

Ajna remembers many lifetimes of soul travels that connect to deep

Vibrate Higher

intuition and reasoning while stimulating the memory. **Ajna** is the Third Eye Chakra, the "Seat of the Soul". Furthermore, it perceives discriminatory judgment within the illusionary field. The understanding is that assessment is perceived through the self and can be changed through the self. Observing the self through the Third Eye gifts fundamentals to inner travel and the unexplored. This vast knowledge relates the outer world to the inner world through Higher Vibrational Consciousness.

The **Sahasrara** Chakra energy travels up to the Third Eye which is found a few inches inside the middle of our forehead. Eventually, it forms a crown of energy that circles back to the base of the spine. The serpent's activation, through the cerebral hemisphere, allows the entire body to function as the spiritual body through transcendental consciousness. Opening up the Chakras, and using the spiritual body's energy, is guided due to the intense power of the body's vibration. Lower vibrations are incapable of activating the serpent energy, the Nadis and the Chakras.

Racism, discrimination, hate, bigotry, anger, fear, and the mistreatment of Nature are powerless through the inner light. However, these feelings all surface through the Chakra emotions, awakening awareness and perception for Vibrating Higher. When vibrating higher, one sees all humans and animals as children of Nature and respects every human of different upbringing, religion, and culture. There is no judgment.

The power and motions of the Chakras are hardly identical. Many experiences are explained as warm light traveling throughout the body which reflects the microcosm. It is further enhanced by astral travel. Each location entered, carries the soul-print's fundamental wisdom that is mastered before moving up and circulating back. There is no time-frame for activating each Chakra. **Feed, move, charge and observe the outer body, and inner spiritual field.**

There is a deeper calculation of the Petals that power the human energy center. The thousand-petaled Lotus, at the **Sahasrara** Chakra, is not exactly 1000 petals. It is multiplied by 1000 petals. The sum of **Muladhara, Svadhishthana, Manipura, Anahata,** and **Vishuddhi** Chakras is 48 petals. The **Ajna** Chakra has 2 petals and is represented by the number 96. When we take the sum of 48 petals and times it by the 2 petals of **Ajna** (Third Eye Chakra), the product is 96 petals. This demonstrates that the power of this Chakra is two times more powerful than the lower five Chakras. **Sahasrara** is the most powerful Chakra. It incorporates the 48 petals of the first 5 Chakras and the 96 petals of **Ajna,** which totals 144 petals. **Sahasrara** is 144 petals times 1000 petals of energy, which powers the Third eye, and the body to **144,000 petals of energy, traveling in 72,000 directions.**

Enter the energy fields and frequency vibrations with a humble heart. The ego does not allow energy to flow. Humbling oneself will help to ascend energy. Higher Vibrations are cloned energies. Sitting in silence in the realms creates self-similar vibrations to reach the **Sahasrara** Chakra.

Repeat the importance of this sacred task. From the moment you were born, you have mastered the use of your Chakras. Through preconditioned programming, this natural phenomenon has been calcified. Vibrating Higher is a massive accomplishment away from societal programming. **Understand your Light, Love, and vibrations. It is time to reconnect, time to retake charge. Follow patterns as they will reveal the signs of frequencies and Love. May it always echo to Vibrate Higher!**

Vibrate Higher

Vibrate Higher every time
Vibrate Higher to the signs
Vibrate Higher take me in
Vibrate Higher light within

Take your time
Yeah every time
And follow patterns
For the signs
Have a humble heart when you go in
Your Compass is the light within

Let this feeling flow
Let it amplify the world
This is energy that grows
When I Vibrate Higher with you

You are not alone
I can help you reach your zone
When this frequency is cloned
I will Vibrate Higher with you

It is time
Time to reconnect
Time to retake charge
Time to vibrate everything
Everything ever so far

Once you're sitting in the realm
Seeing others meditate
You will
Question everything
Concept time invented late
Yet it is time that has made you late
A time that gave you your faith

String the Love
Spin the light
Give the day
A State of night
What's impossible
Is possible
You're the energy
Vibrate comfortable
They will limit you
So become aware
Don't let them tell you
What is atmosphere
When you're in the realm
You'll overhear
There's no language
All of that will disappear

But you'll understand
What it wants from you
As it's telling you
What it really wants from you
You will Vibrate Higher

Vibrate Higher

To the things it wants from you
The fulfillment of your work
Will complete you through
No one understands
Unless they will vibe with you
On some other level solo
Is required from you
It's not meant to stagnate
Or the power dies with you
You will vibrate to the frequency
Inside of you

Let this feeling flow
Let it amplify the world
This is energy that grows
When I Vibrate Higher with you

You are not alone
I can help you reach your zone
When this frequency is cloned
I will Vibrate Higher with you

Yeah we're gonna Vibrate High
Spread the frequency
Until the day we die
Use the energy of people that decide to split
On their mission
And we're gonna get it, get it lit
Luminescence from the heart
Is more of what we need

Vibrate Higher

Spreading of the light
Is where we disembark greed
There's Abundance of this food
We have all these mouths to feed
If your light is vibrant
You know you should take the lead

It is time
Time to reconnect
Time to retake charge
Time to vibrate everything
Everything ever so far
Once you're sitting in the realm
Seeing others meditate
You will
Question everything
Concept time invented late

Yes take your time
Take your time
Take your time, yeah every time
Follow patterns, every pattern
As they will reveal the signs
When your humble heart is true
The journey travels deeper in
Your Compass is the light
The light that lives within

Vibrate Higher

Node 12

Euphoria

~Goddess, take me with you~

*H*umans are spiritual beings with spiritual minds and this wisdom prevails. After all, humans were born with magnificent gifts of spirituality through gratitude, empathy, and Love. When the body is nurtured as a sacred shrine, with appreciation for all it does effortlessly, it will honor the self as a deity. Through this recognition, Euphoria is discovered as a layered state of intense happiness. Within this state of happiness, humans are "royalties" sitting in regal silence with their "in-majesty". Sitting in silence allows observation of the inner body's experiences through actions and feelings. Humans master power over the body. The inner-mirror reflects the empowered self. This reflection is visible to the world. The vibration of the empowered self causes an infectious ripple effect.

Heaven lives within the body and is located in the soul. The soul code communicates and transmits light from the toes to the pineal gland. Stillness and surrender allows the body to self-program simultaneously. Self-programming is not a constant for happiness or righteous living. In fact, life progresses as it is meant to. However, the perceptions shift. Surrender allows Love to surface despite the situations at hand. Love is experienced all around. Love is the Euphoric feeling that is multi-layered within the self. This is where feelings of Love are initiated before being shared with another person. Love for another and Love for the self are both non-egotistical openings to the Love layers. Love impacts the creation of the world around the self. Creation comes in the form of new life, planting of seeds, and the ripple effects of worldly innovations that serve the Earth. The patterns of the ripple effect merge with the whole. Optimistic self-conversing is where the voice meets the mind. Voice and mind are perhaps the most crucial exchange of exhibiting guidance within the self. The outcome of "voice-to-mind" is the visual display of present appreciation and gratitude. Pessimistic self-conversing, however, is where the human experiences cloud perception, weakness, chaos, fear, and negative outlooks. Optimism and pessimism ripple expansively. It is not always easy to remain optimistic when it feels like the walls are closing in. The self should not hide behind pain and sorrow bypassed by spirituality. It is important to experience optimism and pessimism without invoking spiritual bypass. This self-awareness leads to the observation of one's authentic spiritual nature, and journey. The moment is now and what it offers in the future ought to be embraced through the creation of empathetic patterns.

Awakening can be a breakthrough during our clouded perception.
Recite spiritual mantras using "higher-bit" manifestations such as: **"I am grateful", "I am light", "I am Love", "I am abundant", "I am guided", "I am powerful", "I am eternal", "I am fearless", "I am invincible", "I am enough", "I am healthy", "I am sustained", "I am a magnet to my thoughts that echo", "I am the Universe", "What is for me comes to me", "I surrender to the Divine"... .**

*Vibrating impeccable words are powerful. Their meanings must encompass deep underlying beliefs. The manifestation of the word will not take place unless its fundamental core, when verbally expressed aloud, is felt or believed. The Universe (The Divine, Realms, Brahman, Shiva, Dharma and the thousands of names used throughout history, which describe the unknown) does not speak or understand languages. It speaks and understands **vibrations.***

Countless situations present daily incorporations of "higher-bit" manifestations. Higher-bit manifestations include the intention to prepare a meal mindfully. Food fuels and nurtures the body, mind, and soul code. However, the choice of food can either be accepted or rejected by the body code. Vegetables are connected to earthlings. The acknowledgment of life in vegetables and sharing appreciation of their nutrients, serve as medicine to the body. Vegetables and fruits program codes to cells, blood, and veins. **With each bite of food, express gratitude to the inner-self: "I am grateful for this meal." "This food provides my body with what it needs." "This Earthly intake guides, and elevates me."**

Programming these lines of "higher-bit" codes to the spiritual system activates the soul and body code. **Repeat this practice of gratitude without expectations.** It awakens conscious awareness into variables like the mysterious nature of foods, the exquisite sensorial intricacies of food consumption, and its pure enjoyment.

The activated soul-print will share a multitude of information. The first layers of Euphoria teach the depth of the layer stack which is located in the soul. There is no ultimate feeling to accomplish. Each time, the feeling of happiness is unique, and intensifies as it goes deeper into the soul. The mirror to the soul reflects all the penetrated layers. When humans are in harmony with themselves, destruction becomes a particle that dissolves. This allows us to find all-encompassing beauty when traveling through the microcosm. This is an unknown but ineffable journey. The energy of Love releases and creates "Euphoric inner layers". It provides empathy for self, and others that amplifies, recharges, and reactivates ancient universal knowledge. This ancient universal knowledge is the Akashic records. Clouded perception slowly becomes obsolete.

The sleep-wake cycle kicks off daily activities, such as speaking, sitting, walking, running, cycling, driving, working, and engaging with the energies of the outer world. These activities are conscious opportunities for meditation amongst the vast array of minuscule activities humanity partakes in. There is an inherent high to be felt without the use of a substance. It is a feeling of being buzzed through meditation. Humanity's time on Earth is to observe the ultimate benefit of the Earth suit in stillness and in movement. It is through this pursuit that humanity finds the endless gateways which connect to everything. Gratitude creates tranquility which polarizes the magnet to manifest, and corroborate the untrained state. This magnet is the self-similarity of thoughts. The energy of Love spirals effortlessly with the universal spiral. Carefully and consciously, it navigates the Euphoric layer stack. It is where the soul activates, and feeds itself.

Hail to your higher self, surrender to YOU. Euphoric inner layers travel deeper with YOU.

Euphoria

Goddess every moment you are here
I'm living dreams
Dancing timeless into space with you
Fulfills my needs
Like we're lovers you hold onto me
You are my shrine
Stay awake forever
For my Earth remaining time
Take me anytime
Take me anywhere
My in-majesty
My Soul
My inner-mirror
Hailing to my higher self
Surrender to you
Euphoric inner layers
Traveled deeper with you

Feeling, feeling, feeling everything
Feeling everything surreal
Feeling travels through my veins
Through every particle of space
There is this feeling within feelings
And this feeling it is good
Wonder if they see me leaning with my head
And see me move
Because I'm reaching ins-and out of states

Euphoria

Euphoria in layered states
She touched me so we elevate
She's taking time to kiss my face
She's breathing
So I let go
She catches me
I catch her
My soul-print merging with hers
Heaven lives within her

Goddess every moment you are here
I'm living dreams
Dancing timeless into space with you
Fulfills my needs
Like we're lovers you hold onto me
You are my shrine
Stay awake forever
For my Earth remaining time
Take me anytime
Take me anywhere
My in-majesty
My Soul
My inner-mirror
Hailing to my higher self
Surrender to you
Euphoric inner layers
Traveled deeper with you

Goddess take me with you

Euphoria

Travel through my body's eye

Dancing words they're leading I

Energizing Love through the eye

Messages through the eye

Self, higher self

Come take me with you

I'm buzzed through meditation

Got me dreaming of you

Euphorically I sit there

Until I can feel you

I've never felt the way

What I feel every moment

Traveled deeper with you

Goddess every moment you are here

I'm living dreams

Dancing timeless into space with you

Fulfills my needs

Like we're lovers you hold onto me

You are my shrine

Stay awake forever

For my Earth remaining time

Take me anytime

Take me anywhere

My in-majesty

My Soul

My inner-mirror

Hailing to my higher self

Surrender to you
Euphoric inner layers
Traveled deeper with you

Node 13

Awakening

~Lead the world free~

$\mathcal{A}$ll species are natural inventors. Empathetic living impacts the decision-making processes which ensue profoundness, and innovation for this civilization. It may seem simplistic to innovate and empower the creation of a harmonized world; however, data has turned human beings into algorithms. Individuals that vibrate energy selfishly and egotistically promote competition amongst each other. The words, "I don't want to be a number" reverberate. Yet, there is a chase and race to a hypothetical finish line. Being "first" matters to the individual seeking this competitive compartment. The things that are deemed important are the things that affect lives. Variables control life in positive and negative ways. The current structure rules, and controls life on Earth; however, it is deleterious. Gaia struggles to naturally protect her inhabitants. Although Gaia is self-healing, the survival of species depends on how well she is treated. Political games and the millions of operations in a complex world create havoc for earthlings. Solidarity transforms the world by encouraging each human to sow their seeds. **Individually, you unlearn and speak Higher Vibrations into existence through actions, words, silence, and innovations.** Individually, you erect the pillars for a new foundation. This new foundation will guide humanity to a new way of living. Complexity will be prevalent while building. **Inert human beings need your empowerment. You are, contrarily, paving a new road to introduce a new school of thought and journey. You are stepping into the power of your birthright.**

Predictable buying and instant gratification sanctions create a convoluted web, and a higher fall from Grace. This form of Grace is felt when the ego is fed. The ego amplifies inner conflict which leads to hostility. The awakened world connects and disconnects at the seat of the governed entity where new generations question, and demand actions for change. An ever-changing planet requires transitioning order. Limitations prohibit some of humanity's necessities such as food, and shelter. Food is abundant in the world. Yet, food is scarce. Nourishment is surrounded by entities, rules, and barbed wire. The pillars of the new foundation would bestow upon every human the freedom of planting and innovation. This would lead the world into a Higher Conscious civilization. Land and all inhabitants belong to the Earth. Even though the Earth does not belong to humans, the land is claimed by humans. Growing food is reigned over, and all aspects of life swirl around monetary wealth, and power. Present avatars are born into a civilization tiering in religion, culture, class, caste, royalty, gender, race, skin color, and disability. These classifications dictate the course of all lives. Sustenance and clean air are not an imminent plan. The governing entity manufactures divisions and wars. Humans that are tiered lower in the classification hierarchy, struggle to maintain necessities.

Innovations are gifted and are intended to grow meteorically for the subsequent rise of human possibilities. Innovations are not to dominate or serve ego-centrism. Regulations that compromise health stagnant growth. Living in empathy and serving unity is more incredible than acquiring income with greed. Empathy and unity are foreign to the mind that chases numbers. When humanity leaves this Earth, nothing dies with them. The naked body completely disintegrates into the soil of Earth but actions, whilst alive, linger forever through future generations. The dance of efforts determines the web that connects families, friends, and the rest of the world. The highest calling for humans is to LOVE, steward, and protect the planet. Each part of the world has resources that complement the next part of the world. These resources weave a web of chain effects for harmony amongst earthlings. The changing of seasons provides different foods from contrasting regions. Co-existence tolerates the differences on the interconnected web. Interdependence honors and assists in raising vibrations as worldlings. The abundance of food and water keeps the body, and soul elevated. In elevation, the beam of light is amplified and becomes salubrious to others. Neurons are unique and are meant to wire the brain to be of service to humanity in unfathomable ways. The inhumane ways of life, lived in different places in the world, affect the entire Earth's vibration. Humankind has yet to understand this effect. Focusing on simple, genuine ascension is arduous when much of the activated vibrations sphere fear. Agony is deemed necessary for those at the seat of "power". Hunger for power and monetary wealth is used to control the "herd". Humanity's Higher Vibrations would descend the impermanence of control to superfluity. Consciousness is priceless wealth. It is difficult to conceptualize a world where positive news outweighs negative news. Ruling with the ego is a captive mindset. The Maya (illusion) of "protecting" countries and lands creates the opposite effect of defense. Defense awakens attack. Land and its resources cannot be owned.

An "army of aid" is Awakening. It awakens the sharing and inventing of capabilities that produce the vibration of joint ventures. Without sharing, suffering extends to its surroundings. This sorrow may linger for generations. When one soul heals, it does so for the entire lineage. When one soul awakens, it reverberates. Reviving the inner light awakens generations. Manifesting this change fires the nodes of light. **You proliferate light to the world. Soul Awakening is enlightenment. Persevere light within the body, and walk your path to liberation. Your Awakening will lead the world to freedom.**

Awakening

Lead the world free

We are awakening
Spreading enlightenment
Hold onto light within
Lead the world free

Lead the world free

We are awakening
Spreading enlightenment
Hold onto light within
Lead the world free

If you mean to speak on Love
Than you should learn to speak it
There's no mix up
If you meant it
Hearts are beating with it
You don't need to back-stab anyone
Just to show it
It shouldn't feel like hatred is a path
Power ruled by the illusions
For their ego
Amplified by combat

Secure leads insecure

So we don't need to stand your way
Awakening solutions
Around the things that you portray
Collectively awake
We'll send vibrations to the beat
Awakening to problem solving
When our rights are obsolete

The freedom of our consciousness
Knows no such thing
We're light
We are the minds to understand
That you vibrate those fights
Your ego has the programmed
Full of hate
With the things that they debate
Their minds you set to infiltrate
Yet We are here
We're wide awake

We are awakening
Vibrate Higher
Lead the world free

We are awakening
Spreading enlightenment
Hold onto light within
Lead the world free

Lead the world by giving seeds to plant
They cannot eat from all those late night rants
Your antics they just have to go
You're letting all the world to know
This leadership is for the show
Spread your wisdom
Vibing Love
For hearts throughout the globe

This land cannot be claimed,
Not by a tie
Not by a robe
Pretend lands don't already scar
To block the foreign from afar
This was the foreign ground to start
Remember that
You claim you're smart

But listen
I know that the here and now
This will evolve
Debasing every human
Interested in picking wars

We are awakening
Spreading enlightenment
Hold on to light within
Lead the world free

Freedom lives where humans radiate

Cessation of the self divided Faith
Finally some given time to Earth
Strip the buildings out of dirt
My pants are folded from my skirt
We are awakening
Lead the world free

We are awakening
Spreading enlightenment
Hold onto light within
Lead the world free

Node 14

Dharma (applied)

~Stand alone, listen, there are answers within~

Look at the beautiful Earth; it triumphs! Nature is speaking. Synchronicities, and "Dharma" permeates. Everything, good or bad, emits a frequency. Repetition of either vibration generates a stronger frequency. Universal self-talk manifests the human experience. Dharma, in its practice state, surrenders to the higher cosmic order, which is called **Ātman,** in Vedantic Hindu philosophy. Dharma, in its surrendered state, connects to the supreme universal consciousness of the Divine, which is called **Brahman.** Humankind are visitors to Earth and sync with Earth's vibrations in the ascension states of the higher-order. Several modalities interconnect to evoke higher states. **Ātman** seeks to activate the untrained, and unaltered state in the body through fasting. It is important to understand that fasting does not work when practiced selfishly. The practice of fasting for self-improvement, gains a greater understanding of the world around the self, with Love. Fasting assists with the focus that is required for the decalcification, and activation of the Third Eye. Repetition of reaching higher states assists with Dharma practice; whereby, the body, mind, and soul codes are in sync, and in harmony. Some code modifiers include bad habits, unhealthy foods, and toxic relationships. Higher Vibrations facilitate the exit of distortions of the world. Foods and habits that invite lethargy to the practices of Dharma, need annihilation. The adaptation of fasting, effortlessly, indicates the readiness to experience the *Ātman (Soul)* to *Brahman (Divine Consciousness)*. Expanding knowledge rids old life patterns and invites the creation of new ones. The practice of ridding old life patterns imparts knowledge to discern relationships. Relationships may embody confusing vibrations. The power to navigate these confusing vibrations, lies in surrendering to the creation or to the removal of connections, as they pertain to relationships. Neurons fire and wire when the body, mind, and soul are in harmony and trust their interconnected processes. Curiosity about the outer world that is invoked by trust promotes deeper understanding and detachment. The roaming senses of curiosity lead the self and create new ways of adaptation. Resilience and understanding of detachment are achieved and mastered through Dharma.

The Universe admires all souls. The human experience is fragmented in moments, and brings forth teachers and lessons. Experiences may conjure fears which indicate that practice is required in the Maya (illusion) of fear. More instinctively, the practice of obsoleting fear activates neurons that are associated with courage. The wisdom of walking the spiritual path is a solo phenomenon. The Universe distributes lessons in constant manifestations of the mind. Mastering the Universe's sacred energy announces the Aura's visibility. The life-force energy of the Aura emits light around all living entities. The Aura syncs its accurate energy with the wind, trees, and plants. Conversely, the aura generates energy through healing.

The mode of fasting is an individual approach that activates ascension. Ascension filters distortion. Every pathway and life experience is unique. Learning and unlearning stem from listening to the self. It follows the sacred teachings of Gaia while loving and connecting through others. The practice of levitating to higher states is non-duality. It is, however, possible to form energetic spheres of elevation with other souls. In doing so, the human vibration ascends while sitting in silence. After all, humanity is oneness. Even if the actions of thinking, speaking, and walking are different, the soul pulse of humanity connects to the entire vibrational field of Earth. Identifying with another person's struggle presents lessons to live in empathy without judgment. When another person's struggle is judged, collective light-workers are considerate of both sides. Collective light-workers understand that even though Avatars travel as individuals in this world, they are unified by the vibrational field. Neurons are powerful and fire through awareness, confidence, and Love. When thoughts are mastered, the increased confidence forms hereditary conscious wealth. This is Dharma applied. Dharma distributes awareness of the soul's vibration. Dharma is Loving and learning that all creation of life is sacred and eccentric. Dharma is serving the biosphere. Fear, sulking, sadness, uneasiness, hate, gossip, and sorrow are emotions that humanity experiences in their lifetimes. Dedicating the self to vibrational elevations, while experiencing these emotions, may lead to spiritual bypass. Healing emotions is through observation and feeling. Dharma is not a state to be deceived. Dharma is truth. Dharma is successfully practiced, and it applies to this dimension through self-similarity. Therefore, permanence is surrendered to its entirety. True happiness lies within, and dances with the self.

Gaia is sacred. All of Gaia is sacred. There is no particular piece of Earth presiding over the next piece of Earth. There is no better neighborhood,

Dharma (applied)

city, state or country. This planet reveals this constantly. Dharma is compromised by nefarious practices such as killings, and the abuse of Mother Earth's land, and resources. It is a high price to pay for the descending human vibration. Dharma in practice respects the humus of Mother Earth. Anything lesser will result in humanity fighting with each other, and eventually gasping for oxygen. Dharma provides the understanding that every human is Love, and vibrates to the Earth's energy. Dharma is thriving on the individual level for interconnected wholeness. It is experiencing every heartbeat as a miracle. Give the best self to the planet, and in return receive unconcealed truth. Take care of fellow earthlings, and respect Earth and all its inhabitants. **Everything lives within, and through you, in equanimity. Dharma is YOU! You are wired through your inner states! Dharma is unconditional Love.**

YOU can breathe now!

Dharma (applied)

Stand alone
Listen
There are answers within
Stronger than your mind
Let those neurons fire growth
Learn to replicate
Your Dharma it will elevate
It will wire inner states

Learn to replicate
Every thought of vibrancy
And the Love for Nature
That you have now
Focus on the gland
So you tune into the frequency
And you will
Vibrate now
Practice everyday
So you can take your inner-self
To reach your higher state now
After taking all the toxins
From your system
Notice that
You can breathe now
You can breathe now
From your core within
You can breathe now

You can breathe now
Through a lightning spin
You can breathe now
You can breathe now
Psilocybin
You can breathe now
You can breathe now

Neurons that fire
They need to get wired
So calm your mind down
So your souls gets admired
The scanning it happens
When you sit down quiet
The louder you are
The less that they will fire
The less you will see
And the less you will hear
The less they can transfer
When you have your fear
The let-go is magical
Sight of a deer
Don't ever feel fussed
You won't mind
You won't care

Stand alone
Listen
There are answers within

Stronger than your mind
Let those neurons fire growth
Learn to replicate
Your Dharma it will elevate
It will wire inner states

Calling everyone to push your power in the air
While we push out fear
Making those aware
Messing with her Earth
Showing how she can appear
Her reason to despair
To taunt your biggest fear
To tell you
She is hurting from the scars
She's broken from the wars
While you want bigger cars
She couldn't hold it back
She crying leaving tracks
We need to give her back
The land is hers
She needs to have it back

Learn to replicate
Every thought of vibrancy
And the Love for Nature
That you have now
Focus on the gland
So you tune into the frequency

Dharma (applied)

And you will

Vibrate now

Practice everyday

So you can take your inner self

To reach your higher state now

After taking all the toxins

From your system

Notice that

You can breathe now

You can breathe now

From your core within

You can breathe now

You can breathe now

Through a lightning spin

You can breathe now

You can breathe now

Psilocybin

You can breathe now

You can breathe now

Stand alone

Listen

There are answers within

Stronger than your mind

Let those neurons fire growth

Learn to replicate

Your Dharma it will elevate

It will wire inner states

Node 15

Solitude

~Solitude has taken me, powered all this energy~

Life and Love may occur in a whirlwind. Journeying life with someone else is inevitably complicated. Humans meet, connect, and exchange energies. However, they often disconnect their energies before the exchange becomes complicated. Life and Love may also just observe, and choreograph a slow dance. In all possible life and Love scenarios, however many there might be, it is all in divine time. Every type of human connection is a chapter in a lifespan story. The story of the human experience is a manifestation of each person deciding individually when the chapter ends. Humans encounter soulmates and soul-passers. When the connection presents itself as a soulmate, it teaches Love, patience, and non-duality. When the connection presents as a soul-passer, it teaches lessons about life, duality, and the self. All connections are not free of dilemma or trauma. After experiencing lessons, a new vibration awakens.

It is the gift of Solitude. Aloneness allows reflecting on the human experience. Aloneness is not to be confused with loneliness. On the contrary, Solitude is a state of awareness, nature, the self, tranquility, and the activation of the brilliant mind in silence. Self-consultation is distorted when the outer world interjects their opinions. The distorted inputs of the outer world are a point of view. Misunderstandings and biased opinions cloud perceptions and affect the mind capriciously. When the mind, body, and soul discover a higher-bit state of silence, celestial guides awaken. Celestial awareness and guides elevate consciousness. When consciousness awakens, the highest self leads to persistent elevation.

Trauma codes in the body require time to heal, and time to find the inner voice of self again. This voice will present as a wave of new beginnings. Solitude is the wave of new beginnings. Solitude will gift moments to freely express self-love. Healing is a solo journey. Broken hearts are open wounds and emotional weapons. In its healing process, broken hearts may cause damage to other hearts, when rushed into new connections. Healing necessitates a new form of fasting. This would include fasting from chasing and fasting from the rush of instant gratification. These forms of fasting operate as a slow node and ground the self into "being". This process entails embracing, and feeling through the pain of the broken heart. This would enable the broken heart to cycle through the unpleasant moments, and mend its wounds. "Dormancy" heals the broken heart so it may Love again. Complete control and trust in Gaia is surrendering to the stillness of "being". Inner work is the healer when the body is in distress. Mother Earth gifts this state of peace. The inner work promotes less controlling, and more trusting thoughts. Moving into celibacy harnesses a tremendous amount of power. It may seem impossible, in thought, for a person who is longing for touch, and comfort. However, inner work allows the body to experience the energetic reloading of pleasure. The surrender to seclusion replenishes and reloads energy for Higher Vibrations for subsequent intimacy. Intimacy is, after all, a sacred energy exchange. Lack of intimate-node-wiring creates distrust. Dishonesty and lower vibrations while intimate, permeate the body.

Energy is not to be underestimated. In Solitude, communication operates at its highest peak using telepathy. Telepathy is speaking through sacred inner-vibrations. It operates on neural nodes which send messages that are invoked by cosmic influence and vibrations of the Universe. Celestial guides provide incoming and outgoing energy through the human experience. Noise cancellation overtakes the outer layer and processes

143   *Solitude*

clear messaging through the inner layers. These messages ignite constant gratitude for daily tasks and awareness. The practice of gratitude assists in the navigation of life. Trauma may still try to shock the system. However, the awareness of trauma dismantles its grandness, and attempts to heal from the roots of the wounds. Wounds heal with the arrival of new daylight and comforting night cycles. Solitude, practiced over long periods, forms a sacred relationship with the self. Growth, healing, and vast comprehension are the new soul connection to this adventure.

Solitude awakens Nirvana. Achieving the longevity of Nirvana in Solitude is done through the practice of Third Eye Awakening. The creative purpose is understood through rest. Rest is creation. Dreams produce the creative realm. The creative self is lifeless without rest. Where would it find the energy? Where would it find Higher Vibrations without rest? Growth is a surrendered state and cannot survive predictions and expectations. This task may be difficult for predictions, expectations, and planning. Nirvana cannot be planned, but it is nurtured through Growth. Predictions achieve some results, but without projections, everything is possible.

Adapt to change swiftly. Love the moments in silence. Thoughts of being sidetracked or feeling defeated by the world are far away, perhaps

Solitude

dissipated. View the world from the perspective of a new enlightened human. A luminous vibration is present. Vibrations recognize self-elevation and healing. There is complete silence to be activated in the heart and mind. The surrender to Gaia has once again wired nodes and healing vibrations to the World. Vibrate Higher through the thousand-petaled lotus. Vibrate higher with an easy flow through mastered experiences in Solitude.

Solitude is calming every molecule while we're letting Mother Earth take control.

Solitude

Fighting and hiding
My Love's
Gone with the bitter no
Since then I'm Vibrating Higher
With an easy flow

No more living with the humans
That will clearly give me nothing for my growth
A bitter no
Powered by myself and every Goddess
While we celebrate the higher self
And inner glow
Rising from the moments
When we see right through the signs
And things we know
Solitude is calming every molecule
While we're letting Mother Earth
Take control

Fighting and hiding
My love's
Gone with the bitter no
Since then I'm Vibrating Higher

With an easy flow

Gone with the bitter no

Never will I need to hear your bitter no
When did you own my soul?
I really can't remember
What had made us whole
Rising from your control
Solitude is clearly knocking on my door
Sending you this healing from the core
Hoping that you never hurt your lovers anymore

Solitude has taken me
Powered all this energy
Follow all my dreams for real
Who knew that this would be me
Thank you for the things that you have done
I wish you deepest healing from the sun
And when your energy is low
I'll vibrate higher for you
Till you feel like
You've reached back to the sun

Fighting and hiding
My love's
Gone with the bitter no
Since then I'm Vibrating Higher
With an easy flow

Gone with the bitter no

Love's gone with the bitter no
Gone with the bitter no

Solitude

Love's gone with the bitter no

Vibrate Higher

Fighting and hiding

Vibrate Higher

Node 16

Release

~I know you carry pain around, from times that you have been let down~

$\mathcal{E}$verything in the Universe conspires with cosmic order and creates new conditions. Life is not guaranteed. Birth and death are the only inevitable conditions gifted. Each moment in between is a unique snapshot of time, within timeless spirals. Life is lived through feelings such as joy and grief. When grief is experienced, it programs on the last trauma code layer. Therefore, observing and feeling deeply heals all trauma codes.

R.N.K.

There was no intention to mention personal experiences when I started writing the words for *Housing Higher Consciousness - Vibrate to 360 Senses*. However, it is only through experiences that I can reveal my feelings and connect with yours. My soul work is an ongoing journey and the lifework forthcoming from my travels attest to it. However, it is only through the experience of grief that I can understand the feeling of Euphoria. For me to have an understanding of the cycle of birth and death, I had to personally face and experience the pain of loss. For years I have lived in Solitude with my dog, Tipsy Kay. Tipsy was born in 2004 on a farm in Everdingen, The Netherlands. His Jack Russell dog mother barked heavily at me when I visited the barn. It was his first few weeks on Earth. His dog-mom was well aware as to who had arrived to take her puppies away. This experience was over sixteen years ago. The animal realm called my soul to find Tipsy. Amongst little lambs, sheep, piglets, and puppies, a little brown puppy walked over to me, dropped his cares, and fell asleep right between my feet. I picked him up and held him close to my heart. This puppy adopted me. Little did I know that this puppy would travel with me across continents. Tipsy was a bundle of light in my life. We have explored and experienced countless adventures throughout our time together. After 15 years of life, Tipsy became weak. He departed from his animal avatar on a full moon. He lives through me now, and I have our legacy of adventures to live by. Tipsy, intentionally and consciously, exited his body while gifting me weeks of messages that prepared me for his departure.

We are never truly prepared for the hurt that comes from losing someone, and no one's personal experience ever quite stacks up to how painful it truly is to lose a pet. Those that have encountered the blessings of the unconditional and unspoken Love from the incredible animal realm, can agree that the Love we receive from animals is wholesome and truly unconditional. I was inept at handling the forthcoming struggles that accompanied the decisions on whether to put Tipsy to sleep or to take him home. I felt defeated by taking advice from those around me. All I understood was that I needed to surrender and Release. Looking back at my decisions, I am grateful for listening to my heart. I consciously turned away from the opinions shared by those surrounding me. I listened to my heart and the vibrations Mother Nature shared. In my journal, I had written, *"Mother Earth, I ask you for guidance. Please take my Tipsy when he is ready to go. Please guide me."* Watching my Tipsy struggle those last moments was not painless. However, knowing that my surrender to Mother Nature would set him free, held me in comfort. Mother Earth is the decision-maker within Nature. Against all advice, I took my Tipsy home after his last veterinarian visit. Those two days that followed are still painful to replay and express. At 2:27 am on August 3rd, Tipsy Kay was summoned back to the animal realm through the chanting of the *Tibetan mantra of the Medicine Buddha.* This chant was shared with me by my Aunty, twice within one month, which sparked guidance to play this hymn. Being one with Nature helped me to understand the signs. Tipsy needed release from his Earth suit through natural vibrations. There was no other way. Listening to my heart and body helped me to make difficult decisions. Today, I have learnt a lesson on Releasing. I have received the gift of Peace. While writing this Node, I am counting six full moons since Tipsy Kay departed from his avatar. The work will always be and is still an ongoing curriculum of practice and application in guidance and Release.

Grief is a strange concept which arrives in many layers and stages. The only way to deal with it is to surrender and Release it. No one holds answers and nothing will make it easier. Waking up some days comes with more strength than other days. There is no timeframe for healing. Some proclaim that speaking helps while others declare aloneness helps. Whatever stages are mapped out, it would require surrender, feel and Release. Grief extends the energy from which new things can flourish. Death reveals that the avatar of earthlings has a limited time here on Earth. Therefore, live every moment with Love and empathy. This practice will Release Loving and empathetic energies into the realms. Grief also has ugly stages where anger and resentments play a role. **For grief to transition to the next stage, feel through it, so you may benefit from the flourishing fruits of that labor.** This labor is difficult but necessary. Life equals death. The acceptance of death and the work performed during "loss" aligns with cosmic order. The world thrives together with the Release of negativity. The world thrives when it heals together and raises the human vibration. Earthlings that emit effulgence manifest solidarity.

Although your pain may feel unbearable at times, you should know that you are here at this exact time reading this in perfect, and Divine alignment. You are not alone in your quest for liberation. Millions of light-workers around the Globe are sitting in Higher Vibration awaiting your arrival. Therefore, *Release negativity and Vibrate to the frequency of possibility.*

Release

I know you carry pain around
From times that you have been let down
From this point on release this pain

Ayahuasca
Psilocybin

Release

Tangled in the light of energy
Navigate the dark
Roam the expectations of nature
While glowing in the dark
Waves are picked up
Never say a bad thing to your soul
Be kind and gentle to this body
It's the only thing you own

Release negativity
Vibrate to the frequency
Of possibility
Raise your higher self to strictly high
Sagacious company
Give yourself the peace of mind
Release it all once gracefully
You will only block your energy
With a lifelong enemies

Let them hold on to their anger
If they must
Earth does not pause
When you lack your inner trust
Others will project their fear back on to you
Release it
As it has nothing to do with you

Release negativity
Vibrate to the frequency
Of possibility
Raise your higher self to strictly high
Sagacious company
Give yourself the peace of mind
Release it all once gracefully
You will only block your energy
With a lifelong enemies

I know you carry pain around
From times that you have been let down
From this point on release this pain

Ayahuasca
Psilocybin

Release it right now
All the trauma stored to memory
Release it right now
For my ancestors and warriors

Release it right now
For the times I could not catch my breath
I'm breathing right now
It's as much as you allow the past
Release it right now
Feelings merely are the visitors
Release it right now
Take a moment so you understand
Your breathing right now
Control this as it will tell you
To go deeper right now
Your conscious-self is powered through
The activation right now

Release

Release negativity
Vibrate to the frequency
Of possibility
Raise your higher self to strictly high
Sagacious company
Give yourself the peace of mind
Release it all once gracefully
You will only block your energy
With a lifelong enemies

I know you carry pain around
From times that you have been let down
From this point on release this pain

Release

Ayahuasca
Psilocybin

Node 17

Growth

The soul-print is the activation portal to the primordial sound. The soul can beam the depth of where Shiva's drum resonated its first reverberations. This is the primordial sound of the Universe that is known as *"OHM"*. While the celestial bodies vibrated into existence, Shiva awakened in conscious awareness. Celestial guides assisted in the creation of universal receptors. The soul is consciousness and the body is fractal consciousness. **This is not a story. This is a phenomenon that is taking place around and within you.** The vast understanding of the primordial sound is written in the soul code. Celestial influence is awakened by using both stillness and vast creation. They simultaneously provide healing through the primordial sound. The paths to the primordial sound resonate at higher vibrational frequencies. Growth enlightens the domain of neural receptors for conscious wealth. Conscious wealth recollects the soul code.

Worldlings have the ability to understand the manifestation of the mind and all entities that vibrationally form the wholeness of the Universe.

Yin swirls *Yang.*

Within light there is dark. Within dark there is light.

Prana swirls *Akasha.*

Prana is energy and Akasha is "ether".

All matter consciously exists through ether. *Prana* is the beginning of the omnipresence of *Akasha.* The fractal body moves with energy and Growth within *Akasha. Prana* manifests the activation of the *Akashic records.* The fractal body is thus a repository for the manifestations of the *Akashic records.* All universal thoughts that are stored in the spiral gateways of the *Akashic records* belong to Universal Consciousness. Conscious Growth vibrates into the entirety of Universal Consciousness. Conscious Vibrations adhere to the *mind, understanding,* and the *sense of self.* It further extends to the elements of *Earth, Water, Fire, Air,* and *Ether.* These account for the *eight manifestations of human nature.* Together, these eight manifestations

159   *Growth*

construct the spiritual being as the *"House of Higher Consciousness"*. **The primordial sounds have resonated through many forms of molecules to reach your body. These sounds reverberate through you consciously. Therefore, you must live truthfully, and honorably to yourself.** In doing so, the Growth of mind, body, and soul is in conscious elevation. Growth is becoming the trusted and highest version of the self known to date.

You are a humble messenger of Universal Consciousness. Harnessing the ability to use the human vessel, in its ascending vibration, resonates *OHM.* **Trauma codes and obstacles have provided lessons to Grow resilient in your vessel.** Every version of the Avatar evolves. Growth is a manifestation and a message that nothing ever remains the same. Life is a phenomenon that inevitably Grows. **The acceptance of constant Growth allows for the Divine to speak through you. The celestial guides await your presence.**

Level up your Higher Consciousness.

Growth

What You should learn from this
Heaven is right now
There is no loneliness
Aloneness is the remedy to grow through this
Healing will require for our souls to kiss
Giving all of me to
Level up your Higher Consciousness

Level up your Consciousness

I can tell you this,
When you stagnate your Growth
Ostentatious to the world and you will never know
Crisis to the consciousness
No energy reload
Caution with your brain wires connected to the node

Prana swirls Akasha
Energy galactic
Back to vibrating your 360 senses
Solely I'm vibrating
Yet we are connected
Ever so the same
Let this Growth be projected

I will Grow through this
There's no loneliness

Straight up confidence
Ready for the turbulence

Magic to the bone
I'm Growing
Reach my state here all alone
Becoming
Shining out all on my own
Strikingly the path of nothing that I've known

Aloneness is the remedy
To Grow through this
Healing will require for our souls to kiss
Giving all of me to
Level up your Higher Consciousness

What You should learn from this
Heaven is right now
There is no loneliness
Aloneness is the remedy
To Grow through this
Healing will require for our souls to kiss
Giving all of me to
Level up your Higher Consciousness

I will grow through this
There's no loneliness
Straight up confidence
Ready for the turbulence

I've built myself up from my pain
Lifted to the higher sound
No more ego in this life
Dancing on my Goddess ground

Spiral of life, primordial OHM
2.5 million pyramid stones
2.5 million sun years away
The tree of our lives
Does not know of delays
Growing through hurt
Will form what needs to stay
Roots of our tree will grow stronger by day
The seasons will sentiment flowers to trees
It's Love through Third Eye dimensions you'll see

What I have learned from this
Heaven is right now
There is no loneliness
Aloneness is the remedy
To Grow through this
Healing will require for our souls to kiss
Giving all of me to
Level up your Higher Consciousness

Growth

Node 18

Freedom

~Freedom in my mind~

The Universe is experienced within the self and this marvel is referred to as the microcosm. **Freedom brought you here. You have surrendered, and through unlearning, you have reached the base of the mountain.** Surrendering has awakened an ego-less self that can climb the highest of mountain peaks. **What awaits at the peak, is the embodiment of a macrocosmic embrace, and the array of countless mountains, yet to climb.** This represents the endless, unfolding layers of consciousness. The ego-less self has the ability to recognize that everyone is worthy of empathy and understanding.

In humanity, families serve as the foundation of their connection to the world. There may be endless situations in which entities may not agree. There are, however, multiple absolutes such as the arrival of the Avatar, the journey with other Avatars, and the departure of the Avatar. Without an ecosystem, humanity cannot exist. This is also an absolute. Religion or caste is not absolute. Humanity has the ability to live empathetically regardless of differences in religious affiliations, race, and socioeconomic status. The heart is aware of the possibilities that connect to the source. Yet, many humans claim absolute truth in their convictions. Multiple roads lead to unity through different perspectives of life on Earth. A conscious civilization can only be achieved in the absence of pain, suffering, provocation, holy crusades, misogynistic ordinance, racism, child abuse, human trafficking, sex trafficking, murders, political dictatorship, and wars. The sacred knowledge of a conscious civilization was gifted through the soul code. Reading this, here and now, is no coincidence. **The Freedom of the soul is calling.**

Earth has gone through billions of years in cycles of time. Despite the understanding that life is not forever, human civilizations indoctrinate in forgetting the self. The quest to "purchase" celestial bodies explains the Maya (illusions) of the slave race. The "miniature inhabitants" of the land devalued planet Earth's valuation in man-made currencies. The human race aspires to populate celestial bodies while neglecting the responsibilities for their disasters created on Earth. Earth is home to earthlings. When life is departed, the story ends and awakens elsewhere. Freedom in magnitude will elevate civilizations to feed, house, and Love in Solidarity. The power that is unleashed from the gift of freedom is incomprehensible to humankind. The desire for Freedom propels human beings to create a harmonious world. Liberation is observed in stillness where change is inevitable. The openness to change vibrates and elevates an empathetic, unified world. Empathy is growing collectively and amplifies the power within. Solidarity can serve the world, feed the children, overthrow the caste, and dismantle the commanded mindset. Souls go through one life cycle at a time. The mission is to house the highest form of consciousness, at its highest vibration, in this cycle of life. In this cycle, Gaia's soil facilitates healing.

Freedom lives where humans radiate light. The paths are traveled together, in solidarity. It requires reprogramming of current algorithms that oppress through atrocious, aged rules. Predictable behaviors create constraints which cause the brain to think it resides in captivity. The world is held hostage by hierarchies, caste systems, religious ambiguities, and inhuman rules. These systems understand programming and mind-bending. They have learned from energy systems, and are advanced in using it for manipulation. Life-code patterns unlock birthright practices. These practices are Love and empathy for each other. Light-workers are gifted to serve the collective mission. The marvel of the microcosm manifests every need in life. Awakening the ability to help others elevate through conscious vibrations. The light-worker elevates when detached from predictions. Healing gateways beam light that guides the light-worker. Through ascension, Freedom is manifested. Freedom lives in Loving. **Freedom is the constant manifestation of your mind and building your power therein.**

Freedom

Nothing can give us
The time back to win
Blood on their hands
We don't carry those sins
Calling new worlds
Wipe colonial grins
Freedom is building
This power therein

Cause I'm in control of me
And I will take care of me

Freedom in my mind
Freedom
Spreading through this time
Freedom
Governed minds don't live
Prison
Cognitive bridge
Freedom

Freedom is this world
Where no laws' negative effect
Where food is distributed
Without a human form neglect
Where religion is no division
But a celebrated cake

Sharing Love for every difference
And we walk around awake

Freedom from
Giving monthly ties
Increasing ownership of me
Through promises and lies
Mother Earth
Her food is free
And the medicine
She grows
But when we have no liquids
We go sick
We're hungry and
We're broke

If you're going to govern
Take care of everyone
Feed everyone

Nothing can give us
The time back to win
Blood on their hands
We don't carry those sins
Calling new worlds
Wipe colonial grins
Freedom is building
This power therein

We're still staring at colonial grins
While they take
Take our health
Our peace
Our rights
To choose what is good for us
We go against each other
Where we need to unite
They give us pills and wars to control us
We're navigating in this simulation
Caring is freedom

Your freedom is a lie
Oppression is the law to
Chronically stress us
Until the day we die
If laws would help us eat
We wouldn't have no breaking
Through laws
And minimum waging
While their power is there staging
And some people
Yes they think
That without governed lands
Energy roads and water
Would not be running through land
And people would be raging
Yet the sole invention
Of these things

Brought to you
By those of zero governed
In the making

We need to keep inventing
To power each other
Completely mute the governed mind
And live in solidarity

Nothing can give us
The time back to win
Blood on their hands
We don't carry those sins
Calling new worlds
Wipe colonial grins
Freedom is building
This power therein

Cause I'm in control of me
And I will take care of me
They cannot contain their wealth
If we're living free
Through our higher self

Node 19

Soul Sex (practice)

~Touch my heart~

$\mathcal{H}$igher Consciousness is an intimate state where the self resides. The soul carries out work that elevates self-awareness, self-love, self-trust, and confidence. When these "being" states magnify, the soul is reflected in mirrors in multifarious forms. This awakening brings forth the law of soul attraction, and connection. The experience is magnetic. In various states of *Housing Higher Consciousness,* a multitude of Love connections gravitate divinely, and unexpectedly to the activated soul code. The connected souls surrender to the microcosm and gravitate to each other. All Soul connections must surrender to divine timing and order to encounter each other. On the other side of surrender, is restlessness. Restlessness attracts the identical vibration that is reflected. Unfolding restlessness invokes lessons, and the yearn manifests transient connections. Restlessness will manifest in human form. The state of surrender and exterior influence signal the soul, and power the vibration of self-trust. The heart is able to precisely feel "who" has entered the vibration. The vibration "senses" the soul that has entered as either a soul connection, soul lesson or soul passer. The inner voice guides from within the vibration. It is easy to fall into the superficial layers of "Love". It is phenomenal to feel wanted and to be showered with adoration. It strokes the ego. The early stages of Love are precious. The journey starts with the prettification of a Love story and deep sentiments of matrimonial bliss. It is beautiful when it happens. The soul is, however, always inhibited to connect beyond the superficial layer. The soul programs the Avatar. Once the connection to "self" is unearthed, Soul Sex is discovered. Soul Sex is the practice of ego-less self-love.

Solitude is a dedicated effortless practice that commands "effort". Soul Sex is a state where the self resides solo. The self is in trusting and higher vibrations where immense self-awareness is present. This experience elevates self-trust for soul connections to appear in divine timing. Deep state meditation releases various forms of sexual energy in the body. Intimate thoughts and touches are merely ways to experience climactic pleasures. A climax can present in many other ways. Ultimately, the practice of Soul Sex experiences this climax without "thoughts" or "touches". Soul Sex energy "serpents" through the Chakras effortlessly.

The swiveling serpent energy, which the body has harnessed over time, ascends with intense force. This climactic energy is powerful and requires caution. Remember that mind-body-soul programming is potent and experiences ultimate pleasure through Higher Vibrations. When the body is ready and its energy is harnessed, it allows for the effortless sharing of vibrations using Soul Sex exchange. When the body is not ready and the practice ends prematurely, it results in lower vibrational energy. After all, the soul loves independently and it must master that first. The soul does not undermine, condescend or question self-love. The soul manifests Love and powers the body and mind. Soul Sex does not invite anyone to its circulating vibration. Soul Sex avoids attracting the wrong connection. Energy exchange is venerated as it is sacred and Divine.

The absence of healing energy transcends trauma. Extensive soul healing is required. The act of "making Love" is making Love energy with another person. Energetic vibrations transcend and exchange more than just a "good feeling". Falling in a moment of lust downloads to the repository of energy exchange. Feeling numb and empty after indulging in meaningless soul plunging weighs heavy on the human body. Soul Sex trusts the self. Love that is accumulated by this practice may surface past experiences. Questions that might be revealed are for healing and do not serve to punish the self. Soul work is not easy since the memory recollects downfalls, heartbreaks, shocks, reckless behaviors, shame, and pain. Through evocation, the complex human layer prepares a body that is ready to apply its practiced Soul Sex. This is not an overnight task. The soul elevates to new and unexplored vibrations. Soul Sex is one of the many elevations to practice and to apply *Housing Higher Consciousness.* There are multifarious ways to discover gateways to activate the heart, the soul, and the magic that the body performs. Illumination attracts luminescent souls. The soul creates profound circumstances as it drops deeper into the self. The Soul Sex experience cannot be controlled. The soul emits what it beams, and attracts what is gifted to the self. Soul Sex is an intimate relationship with the self that turns into an effortless lasting relationship. When the self is honored, the soul code attracts soul connections. These connections will elevate soul work, attract soul tribes, and align soul mates. **Forget everything you have read about Soul Sex. Emerge in deeper vibrations of surrender. Soul Sex, in practice, is still always the surrender of the soul to the Higher Vibrational Frequencies of the Universe.**

Soul Sex (practice)

Lifting my body
Di heart she ah try me
She bring di song
She nah deh undermine me
Di feeling she give me
Me can't underrate
She manifest Love
Me nah question di faith
Di song she ah sing
Is di song for di soul
Inviting nobody
Alone in control

Touch my heart
Falling deeper into you
So alive
Penetrating through
With this light
I belong to you
Take me higher
Almost there for you

Soul Sex tonights loving
Teasing, flirting and touching
Rain will be flowing
Bite my lips
You are stunning

Soon to enter vibration
Faster through the foundation
Touching me now
Will flow Love and rain of
Heavenly sweet elevation

Soul sex has me laying in my bed
For days with you
We've been kissing for so long
Our clothes are soaking through
While you have been touching me
I've been touching you
While you have been drinking me
I've been drinking you

Touch my heart
Falling deeper into you
So alive
Penetrating through
With this light
I belong to you
Take me higher
Almost there for you

Lifting my body
Di heart she ah try me
She bring di song
She nah deh undermine me
Di feeling she give me

Soul Sex (practice)

Me can't underrate
She manifest Love
Me nah question di faith
Di song she ah sing
Is di song for di soul
Inviting nobody
Alone in control

Soul sex has me laying in my bed
For days with you
We've been kissing for so long
Our clothes are soaking through
While you have been touching me
I've been touching you
While you have been drinking me
I've been drinking you

Touch my heart
Falling deeper into you
So alive
Penetrating through
With this light
I belong to you
Take me higher
Almost there for you

Lifting my body
Di heart she ah try me
She bring di song

She nah deh undermine me
Di feeling she give me
Me can't underrate
She manifest Love
Me nah question di faith
Di song she ah sing
Is di song for di soul
Inviting nobody
Alone in control

Soul Sex (practice)

Node 20

Soul Sex (applied)

~Love cannot be captured, let it find me~

/his nanoscopic compilation of *Housing Higher Consciousness* has exposed the constant repetition of surrender in many different forms. The soul code guides you to live in harmony as bees do. Higher Awareness and Universal Spiritual Laws elevate the mind, body, and soul. When self-love is observed, it awakens freedom in hearts and movements. The practice of Soul Sex is a commitment that becomes effortless. This describes effortless "effort", which is natural but intentional. The Divine cosmic bodies conspire to awaken the basic laws of life. At a micro level, the Third Eye energy transcends to the macrocosm. At a macro level, the spirals of the Universe transcend to the microcosm. The basic laws of life elucidate "Breath is Wealth". When the body climaxes, the Soul Sex portals transcend energy through the veins, which triggers the five senses to pulsate and gush through 355 unexplored, and unidentified senses.

This may confuse the 5 "down to Earth" senses. For example, when "lusting" after someone, the body experiences a "one time high" which may be followed by a feeling of emptiness. This feeling of emptiness lures the body and mind to experience the "one time high" again. It becomes an addiction after lust. However, when Soul Sex is experienced through aloneness, it surrenders to the inner Divine. This high is magic performed by the body. Magic is not a scientific attestation but the high is guided by the feminine and masculine principle in divine balance. Soul Sex in unity is reciprocated energy and is divinely amplified.

When "seeking" Love, the feeling is found in something that "resembles" Love. This resemblance will be what is perceived as needed or wanted. However, Love can only be experienced at the root level of Love that is known to the self. It is a mirror reflection of how the self is viewed. Love resemblance requires healing before vibrations can be shared again. **"Love cannot be captured, let it find me."**

Feeding the ego invites the inducement of anger. The bitter taste of actions in moments of anger rises from zero to one hundred in seconds. Also, envy and self-sabotage are ego subsets. When these egotistical feelings arise, the soul is called to practice again. Furthermore, this practice will need to start from the zero-point energy field. There is no easy route as this enactment is necessary until it is mastered. Soul passers are temporary connections that teach lessons and enable thoughts for second-guessing. Therefore, it is important to restart from zero-point energy.

There is no definition of Soul Sex. Soul Sex is a combination of self reached states that are achieved as the soul makes decisions for energy exchange. This exchange of energies elevates to Higher Vibrations, which reinforces the release of neurotransmitters in balance, to sincere and higher practices. It is important, as mentioned in previous Nodes, that being an observer to balance is key to unlock higher states. Love guides humankind. Love finds hearts; it is quantified, pure, and accepting. The soul-print is the birth code. This code is "destiny". **Destiny is always on time.** Surrendered Soul Sex awakens true destiny. Feelings that are second-guessed are left behind. Fear dissolves. The heart is ready to share all of the lessons that it has practiced by using energy, which changes rapidly and expands through connection. Energy activates, mushrooms, extends, and exchanges. With Love, a new, carefree pattern is created which progresses to the thickening of the carefree, Love receptors. Love is neogenesis. Love is in tune with the elements of Earth, Water, Fire, Air, and Ether. The body constitutes these elements. Observation of the body's elements should be a regular

Soul Sex (applied)

focus as it teaches about the unknown. The elements are reflective of self-care, self-talk, and the choice of energy invited to hearts, bodies, and souls. Short-lived relationships reveal their expiry through signs in dreams, meditation, and the different forms of synchronicity. The Universe conspires to liberate souls, which in turn, guides. The body stores codes by using its sensors. These codes are the inputs to the collective energy field. Earthlings understand these complexities at the cellular level. Cosmic vibrations are communicating when there is an "off" feeling. This feeling awakens the code of sensory modality.

Don't be hard on yourself. You are clearing yourself from a lineage of conditioning. There is no access point for dismantling conditioning. Dissolution of conditioning happens through the shedding of layers. The nodes reflect that unlearning awakens the genesis of the soul. This state is not meant for the ostentatious world, but for gaining clarity with the human into "being". The body dances wide awake through ether. Humankind is destined for greatness through the genesis of human souls. The mission is always serving through soul-work. This soul-work can be actively participating in the animated world or sitting in meditation to reach souls beyond their physical capacity. Sensory modality is a personal phenomenon but sends waves to listen, observe, and empathize. Wherever

Soul Sex (applied)

a soul print is activated, the hypothetical serpent is awakened, thereby raising the Human Vibration. Humanity walks the Earth simultaneously and shares this planet. Humankind is responsible for each other.

Heal yourself and *Intro* your body to foods that perform *Like Psychedelics.* Remember that you have the ability to destroy the ego, and observe the world in its *Programmed (beyond code)* state. When this state is recognized, reprogramming becomes effortless "effort". You are, and are amongst the *Warriors* that have *Arrived.* Teach the *next-gen Queens and Kings* about Warriors that have arrived throughout time. Become the human that connects to all living beings in this *World of Pulsation.* Support the nurturing *Matriarchy Rising* as they will take care of the planet. Be aware of the rules of the *Binary Human;* they may cloud your perception. Your *Inner Compass* is your wealth; therefore, *(practice) Dharma.* Vibrate Higher through the thousand-petaled lotus. *Euphoria* is achieved in a layered state of *Awakening* through the realms. By following the Universal Spiritual Law *Dharma* is *(applied).* Sit in *Solitude* and *Release* everything that does not serve you. Allow your *Growth* to travel inner worlds, beyond the physical realm. Love and empathize with everyone you encounter as their battles are invisible. *Freedom* lives where you radiate light and through this illumination, the soul vibration opens your gateways to *Soul Sex* in *(practice).* Through these practices, you will find liberation in sharing that which you have accumulated for *Soul Sex (applied).*

Soul Sex (applied)

Vibrate Higher

Soul Sex

Lifting my body
Di heart she ah try me
She bring di song
She nah deh undermine me
Di feeling she give me
Me can't underrate
She manifest Love
Me nah question di faith
Di song she ah sing
Is di song for di soul
Inviting nobody
Alone in control

Soul sex through the veins
Let it find me
Love cannot be captured
Let it find me
Guide me through the realm
Never hide me
Second guessed feelings
Are behind me

Quantifying Love

Through my body
Love is never sold
You cannot rob me
Energy protected
Love is running
Through my body
Soul sex is the only way
That you can find me

Loving alone
Soul Sex
Is higher vibration alone
Climax is pushing
Vibration up high
Giving this climax
High up in the sky
Loving alone
Giving this feeling
With ease all alone
Earthlings must know
How to Love all alone
Quantify Love
Spread it all through di home

Setting the tone
Loving this feeling
I feel all alone
Kissing her slowly
The realm that she roams

Deepened the feeling
To reach cosmic zone

Spreading from my veins
Pumped out through my heart
Spilling on my skin
Glowing in the dark

Leaving traces for returning
To the journey
Through wisdom of the inner spark

Lifting my body
Di heart she ah try me
She bring di song
She nah deh undermine me
Di feeling she give me
Me can't underrate
She manifest Love
Me nah question di faith
Di song she ah sing
Is di song for di soul
Inviting nobody
Alone in control

Focus
Vibrate Higher

I should have probably

Prepared you for
What I'm about to do right now
I'm about to make you feel these drums
In your veins
But let's start with the bass

Lifting my body
Di heart she ah try me
She bring di song
She nah deh undermine me
Di feeling she give me
Me can't underrate
She manifest Love
Me nah question di faith
Di song she ah sing
Is di song for di soul
Inviting nobody
Alone in control

Soul Sex (applied)

$\mathcal{U}$niversal messages are never outdated.

$\mathcal{H}$umanity is one. $\mathcal{O}$ne planet. $\mathcal{O}$ne world. $\mathcal{O}$ne vibration.

$\mathcal{H}$umanity is responsible for raising the Earth's vibration, and

$\mathcal{H}$ousing $\mathcal{H}$igher $\mathcal{C}$onsciousness

in their energetic sphere.

Through this exploration,

the Universal Spiritual Law

abides by the quest to

$\mathcal{V}$**ibrate to 360** $\mathcal{S}$**enses.**

Mantras for Housing Higher Consciousness
and raising the Human Vibration

Mantras for Housing Higher Consciousness

and raising the Human Vibration

Mantras for Housing Higher Consciousness

and raising the Human Vibration

Mantras for Housing Higher Consciousness

and raising the Human Vibration

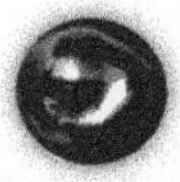

R.N.K.

High-Souled

Beaming Light Codes for Earth

H O U S I N G
H I G H E R
CONSCIOUSNESS

The Awakening of the Serpent

Encoded Vibrations

Uploading to the Universe